Advanced Negotiation Skills
In A Week

Peter Fleming is a Chartered Fellow of both the Chartered Institute of Marketing and also the Chartered Institute of Personnel Development, having been awarded an Oxford Master's in Human Resource Management. With significant retail experience in the UK (marketing and buying) and people development with a UK government agency, he established his own business consultancy group which provides structured learning projects in the UK, Europe and the Middle East.

This is one of several books he has published on negotiation with John Murray Learning, including the predecessor to this title, *Negotiation Skills In A Week* (2016), and *The Negotiation Coach* (2015), the latter of which applies proven development techniques resulting from his pioneering research on improving the effectiveness of management learning.

Advanced
Negotiation Skills
In A Week

Peter Fleming

First published in Great Britain in 2014 by Hodder & Stoughton. An Hachette UK company.

First published in US in 2014 by The McGraw-Hill Companies, Inc. This edition published in US by Quercus.

This revised and updated edition published 2016 by John Murray Learning

Copyright © Peter Fleming 2014, 2016

The right of Peter Fleming to be identified as the Author of the Work has been asserted by him in accordance with the Copyright, Designs and Patents Act 1988.

Database right Hodder & Stoughton (makers)

The *Teach Yourself* name is a registered trademark of Hachette UK.

British Library Cataloguing in Publication Data: a catalogue record for this title is available from the British Library.

Library of Congress Catalog Card Number: on file.

Paperback ISBN 978 1 473 60807 8

Ebook ISBN 978 1 471 80109 9

1

The publisher has used its best endeavours to ensure that any website addresses referred to in this book are correct and active at the time of going to press. However, the publisher and the author have no responsibility for the websites and can make no guarantee that a site will remain live or that the content will remain relevant, decent or appropriate.

The publisher has made every effort to mark as such all words which it believes to be trademarks. The publisher should also like to make it clear that the presence of a word in the book, whether marked or unmarked, in no way affects its legal status as a trademark.

Every reasonable effort has been made by the publisher to trace the copyright holders of material in this book. Any errors or omissions should be notified in writing to the publisher, who will endeavour to rectify the situation for any reprints and future editions.

Typeset by Cenveo® Publisher Services.

Printed and bound in Great Britain by CPI Group (UK) Ltd., Croydon, CR0 4YY.

John Murray Learning policy is to use papers that are natural, renewable and recyclable products and made from wood grown in sustainable forests. The logging and manufacturing processes are expected to conform to the environmental regulations of the country of origin.

John Murray Learning
Carmelite House
50 Victoria Embankment
London EC4Y 0DZ
www.hodder.co.uk

Also available in ebook

Contents

Introduction

So, you are now an experienced negotiator. But what do you understand by that description? Are you a 'fixer'? An intermediary? A person to whom others turn when they need solutions to difficulties with others? Whether or not you see yourself in these situations, your interest in this book (a more advanced follow-up to *Negotiation Skills In A Week*) indicates that you have more than a passing interest in the topic. More importantly, you want to improve the results you achieve from the negotiating process.

When you think analytically about your most recent experiences, you will probably be wondering how to measure your levels of success. After all, a deal done must surely satisfy both sides, or it would have broken down. And perhaps you are feeling 90-per-cent sure that you could not have achieved more.

That last elusive 10 per cent is probably the source of some lingering doubts – and might lead you to kick yourself if it is ever revealed that you could have done better.

But don't panic! The aim of this book is to help you to balance these dilemmas with the need to close deals that will benefit your organization and those you are working with. 'Win/win' is still our principal aim in negotiating, even if it seems a hard standard to achieve!

This week we will help you work through how to:

● strengthen your inner determination and confidence
● choose a preferred negotiating style
● build and fulfil a partnering relationship for the longer term
● analyse opportunities for influencing opponents' organizations
● build and lead a focused negotiating team
● agree the rules of engagement

- use consulting behaviour to uncover problems and ways of achieving movement in a case
- analyse and manage conflict
- avoid embarrassment through failure to close a deal by learning about common mistakes
- celebrate success and plan your future.

At the end of each chapter you will find a multiple-choice 'progress check' designed to test your understanding. (The answers can be found at the back of the book.) Enjoy this personal development programme – all from a week's study!

Peter Fleming

SUNDAY

Preparation: a hard taskmaster

Most negotiators are kept busy pursuing their objectives with little opportunity to:

- 'stop the clock'
- revisit their methods and approaches
- set some realistic development goals.

Even when self-reviews are second nature, the sheer pace of business can make such activities difficult (and, possibly, unattractive).

Today we are encouraging you to begin a self-development journey with a view to handling more demanding projects and achieving an even higher level of success by negotiating even better deals.

After each day try to develop your Personal Action Plan (see back of book) and implement it.

Today you will achieve the following tasks:

- Rate yourself as a negotiator and your relationship with others (and consider the strengths and weaknesses of each approach)
- Obtain some feedback from someone who knows you well (possibly confirming those ratings)
- Learn which styles are most common among top 'win/win' negotiators
- Show that you can produce a negotiation plan with clear goals and objectives
- Reassess your personal communication skills – both verbal and non-verbal – and identify some improvement points.

SUNDAY

MONDAY

TUESDAY

WEDNESDAY

THURSDAY

FRIDAY

SATURDAY

Have you ever met a *real* expert? No, not a self-proclaimed one but someone whose expertise is well known and valued by many people. Would you dare to question this person's word or advice? Probably not, unless you wanted to test their expertise. If this is the case, then read on.

Recognizing someone's expertise should make a negotiation easier – but sometimes it can simply raise the stakes. 'Why don't we let our two experts meet and sort this thing out and we'll simply agree who pays what and when?' Such a proposal should be a simple way out of a difficulty, but there are still enormous pitfalls to avoid – for example:

- **Trial of expertise:** the experts enter into an academic form of arm-wrestling (to prove or disprove theory, academic learning, or even practical common sense)
- **One-upmanship:** one expert promotes their own theories as supreme, with all others deemed worthless
- **Research awareness:** there is a reluctance to recommend a particular route for fear that someone else is already working on this project and is more likely to achieve a successful result more quickly
- **Long grass:** one party seeks to kick the negotiation into the long grass with the aim of delaying any decision until events make the original scheme or idea redundant.

In a theoretical sense, a negotiation takes place between two people or parties who start out in the belief that their knowledge is sufficient for them to debate proposals and arrive at a deal that will benefit both sides (or at least their own!).

How would you feel if your opponent is a novice or has little knowledge of the task in hand? Relaxed? Excited? Suspicious? Sympathetic? Or simply concerned?

After all, it should be easy to achieve a deal in such circumstances, but could that deal be implemented to everyone's satisfaction? What might happen further down the line? Could the other party withdraw, default or go into liquidation? Or just decide to fail to deliver?

This might result in a protracted and expensive legal case – with an ultimate result of lose/lose: on one side the original need still exists while on the other the 'consideration' (money or benefit) remains uninvested.

There is a much better chance of achieving a good deal when both parties are well prepared. This means understanding:

- the technical features
- the 'deliverables'
- the overall terms and conditions
- each party's track record on delivery or implementation
- safety nets in case of future difficulties
- relative power factors (both real and perceived).

If this sounds like a tall order, think how you might feel if, in the process of a negotiation, you suddenly realize that you had shortcomings in your own preparation? What action would you take?

There are four main factors that contribute success to a negotiation:

1 knowledge of the subject/processes involved
2 the relative starting positions of the negotiating parties
3 any levers/benefits that could be applied to bring the parties towards an agreement
4 the skills involved in influencing/persuading the other party to reach agreement.

Confidence comes from sound knowledge, which results from thorough preparation.

So why start this book with yet more exhortations about preparation? In a way, the more experience negotiators have, the greater the risk that they will cut corners in the belief that thorough research, reading and analysis are no longer so essential. It is certainly time-consuming, but expertise is maintained only if it is constantly topped up.

Preparation is a hard taskmaster – unprepared negotiators are vulnerable to making expensive mistakes; they may be clever at improvising or covering them up, but serious

SUNDAY

MONDAY

TUESDAY

WEDNESDAY

THURSDAY

FRIDAY

SATURDAY

errors have a way of resurfacing when the agreement is implemented. Will the 'guilty' party have escaped? Possibly, but their reputation may be sullied. The message is clear – don't let this be you!

This may seem obvious, but negotiations can come to grief when some of the key factors listed are missing and especially when new relationships are being formed. Remember, too, that what is obvious to you may not be obvious to your opponent. What is worse, they may be using a competitive style to encourage you to throw caution to the wind and negotiate spontaneously, with the assumption that this tactic might benefit them considerably more than you.

One solution

If you feel that your opponent does not have the necessary skills to reach a deal with you, then it is always possible to escalate the topic or project to someone at a more senior level, with agreement from your client or supplier that they do the same. To avoid your opponent losing face, you could suggest that your two bosses come to the next meeting to help with the agenda. You cannot, however, make too much of a habit of using this tactic – your own organization may begin to worry that you are not up to the job!

One way of exploring these potential difficulties in advance is to implement an internal dummy run, or role-play, with a senior manager or colleague. The objective is simple – to pinpoint any unidentified obstacles or barriers to an acceptable agreement.

Who should I be?

We shall return to the preparation theme a little later. But first of all, let's conduct a self-examination task of our own values and approaches to negotiation.

TASK 1: RATE YOURSELF – WHAT KIND OF NEGOTIATOR AM I?

Please rate yourself on the following profiles by choosing the number that you believe you portray in all your relationships with others, inside your organization and externally. (1 = does not apply to me and 9 = applies to me most of the time in business deals.)

Role 1: SAFETY FIRST
Your rating: 1   2   3   4   5   6   7   8   9

If you fall into the **Safety First** category, you might err on the side of safety with every decision and negotiation you undertake. In the extreme, you have an extremely cautious approach to risk-taking – always sticking to the verifiable truth and a safe ground that will work out equally satisfactorily in both the short and the long term.

Role 2: OPPORTUNIST
Your rating: 1   2   3   4   5   6   7   8   9

At the other end of the scale, you might be an **Opportunist** – quick to reach a deal that you instinctively know will be welcomed by your own organization, even if you are unsure whether it will achieve much for your opponent.

Role 3: COMPLETER/FINISHER
Your rating: 1   2   3   4   5   6   7   8   9

A **Completer/Finisher** is someone who aspires to have all the *i*s dotted and *t*s crossed and sets out from the start to ensure that everything promised can be delivered exactly as agreed. Fine detail is important to this negotiator as an indicator of both good faith and precision, which is essential for full completion of the contract/agreement.

Role 4: ESCAPOLOGIST
Your rating: 1   2   3   4   5   6   7   8   9

An **Escapologist** boasts that he or she never relies on the 'crutch' of logical thought and instead prefers to cut deals on the basis of instinct. A thrill is gained from living dangerously and the Escapologist may well be tempted to make promises

SUNDAY

MONDAY

TUESDAY

WEDNESDAY

THURSDAY

FRIDAY

SATURDAY

that are just on the right side of the law. Unsurprisingly, these people do experience difficulties with deals, but thrive on the skill of being able to 'pull another deal' that promises to correct the earlier one. They always seem able to recover without any taint to their short- or long-term results... or they move jobs quite frequently! Are you tempted to think like this?

Role 5: POLITICIAN
Your rating: 1   2   3   4   5   6   7   8   9

The **Politician** is very concerned about ensuring that the deal reached meets current standards of acceptability – in terms of preferred status, rules, descriptive terms and/or political norms. These aspects can be allowed to take precedence over what is practical.

Role 6: EXPERT/TEACHER
Your rating: 1   2   3   4   5   6   7   8   9

A true **Expert** is often self-effacing and quiet about their expertise (whether publicly acknowledged or not). Experts can also present themselves as people who know a great deal about most topics and are not reluctant to share their supreme knowledge in everyday conversation as well as in negotiating sessions. They can often be heard explaining things with sentences starting with: 'You know why that is, don't you?' (which precedes a detailed explanation that is mostly accurate but of little interest to the audience because of the manner in which the information has been introduced).

Role 7: EXTROVERT
Your rating: 1   2   3   4   5   6   7   8   9

Warm and sociable, the **Extrovert** enjoys the company of other people and, at the extreme, will only happily negotiate awkward or difficult issues when they can predict that an existing comfortable client relationship will not be compromised.

Role 8: PESSIMIST
Your rating: 1   2   3   4   5   6   7   8   9

A **Pessimist** generally does not make a good negotiator as negotiation is mainly about the future. At the extreme, pessimists appear not to be optimistic that there is even a future ahead. In reality, the pessimism may be a front to minimize opponents' expectations.

Role 9: NAIVE PERSON
Your rating: 1   2   3   4   5   6   7   8   9

You may think that, if your opponent's organization is foolish enough to delegate negotiations to such **Naive** people, then why should you worry if they let you gain a significant win? The issue is that, once a big problem has been solved, the blame games follow. This may lead to attempts to renegotiate or take some spoiling action, making it impossible for the deal to go ahead. In effect, the deal becomes a lose/lose agreement.

Role 10: CONTROLLER
Your rating: 1   2   3   4   5   6   7   8   9

A **Controller** feels the need for personal control of all aspects of a negotiation and, at the extreme, the preparations for, and implementation of, the agreement as well. This may exist through an innate insecurity and fear of the likely repercussions if the deal should go wrong: loss of income/security or tarnished reputation. The Controller will believe that the ends justify the means.

The experienced negotiator will have recognized some – if not all – of these ten styles in colleagues and past opponents. In their extreme forms, each may have a frustrating effect on other people, but can you make them work?

TASK 2: CHECK YOUR RATINGS WITH A COLLEAGUE OR PARTNER WHOSE JUDGEMENT YOU TRUST

The need remains to check our own perception and to set some goals to improve our approach and therefore our results. Ask a colleague to review your self-rating by choosing the rating they feel is most appropriate for you and offering you examples to support any significant variations (of two grades or more).

TASK 3: RATE YOURSELF – WHAT KIND OF PERSON WOULD YOU *LIKE* TO BE?

Is it possible to be all these things all the time? Having rated yourself on these scales, I now urge you to revisit the listing and think about the score you would like to achieve in the future. Given your environment and role, they may not all be higher than your present rating and some of the gaps between current and desired ratings may be rather small, although important all the same.

TASK 4: REFLECTION: 'ALL THINGS TO ALL PEOPLE?'

Another mark of highly skilled negotiators is that they are adept at adjusting their style and technique to fit those of their opponent. To be able to do this successfully, it is necessary to identify typical styles of people with whom you have negotiated. This next task is therefore to revisit Task 1 and identify past negotiators you have worked with. Use the same criteria to rate them on the scale. (It would be best to use pseudonyms if you write their names down!)

We know that any negotiating interview aims to achieve a clearly understood agreement that both sides are committed to implementing. It is sometimes argued that enjoying these meetings is something of a luxury and that the main measure should lie in the resulting agreement and its implementation.

A meeting is usually measured by the objectives that have been achieved, and both parties will be using their skills of influencing and persuasion in order to get a result. So, finally, let us consider the best methods of responding to the challenges offered by some of the extremes of negotiating style that are listed above.

You will have style preferences for all the negotiators you meet from the above listing, but, for the sake of simplicity, we can classify them as follows:

● Class A: Behaviours and styles that are most likely to bring best results
● Class B: Behaviours and styles that may limit your results to just average.

Class A

Role 1: Safety First
One way of breaking this down is by helping the other person to recognize the advantages of a proposed step through highlighting its good points and diluting any objections by expressing the unlikelihood of them occurring and the simple steps that could be taken to get back on track. This style might also be recognized as 'hand-holding'. As negotiators gain more experience and achieve some successes, this style tends to be overtaken by other styles.

Role 2: Completer/Finisher
People in this category generally seek the highest results from regular negotiations, in the sense that their results are usually sound, with rare errors or exceptions. Their agreements are usually fulfilled 100 per cent and, should any 'failures in implementation' occur, they are corrected (or compensated for) very rapidly. Natural reactions may include Safety First or even Controller.

Role 3: Expert/Teacher
Resist the temptation to compete with this strategy, keeping conversation factual and based on the current case. If necessary, ask how examples quoted relate exactly to the deal under discussion, indicating where factual evidence departs from the parallels quoted. If progress is being made, reinforce the benefits of arrangements that are proposed.

Role 4: Controller
Even if you find this style irritating, the best reaction is Safety First as it seeks to convince the opponent that all requirements have been, or will be, met.

Role 5: Opportunist
Taking a Safety First style with an Opportunist can generate considerable frustration because the Opportunist may see any obstacles (even open questions) as being used as a barrier. The Opportunist may be motivated by timing and will respond to phrases such as 'It's now or never' or 'We'll miss the boat if we have to go through the fine detail'. If you fear that your preparation is not 100 per cent, then seek to delay the meeting until it is. Try to neutralize the pressure by asking careful questions and demanding factual answers that compare with your preparation favourably. In extreme, rigid cases, walk away.

Class B

Role 6: Escapologist
The preferred response would be Safety First or Controller. However, experienced Opportunists may take some risks with Escapologists, especially where the risks are strictly limited and could be readily recovered (in a retail setting, for example, where an inexpensive product could bear a considerable reduction to its selling price as a crowd puller for the first day of a sale).

Role 7: Politician
The role of Politician is a tempting opposition role to take but this may result in a considerable investment of time and patience in pursuit down various blind alleys. Resist the temptation to try to change the accepted modus operandi: go along in the role as another Politician – while learning from the process and making careful note of opportunities for streamlining it.

Role 8: Extrovert

Notable for the style of talking too much, the Extrovert may unwillingly give away vital bargaining information without obtaining anything in return. Ask more questions with the aim of restricting the conversation to the negotiation in hand, and try to resist engaging in storytelling and socializing: fun and laughter should not play a significant role in the negotiating process. The best move is to agree to take time out to celebrate the deal *after* it is achieved, not before.

Role 9: Pessimist

Use the Expert role to illustrate the benefits to be gained and provide protection in the Completer/Finisher role.

Role 10: Naivety

An obvious reaction is the Expert/Teacher role but, if you choose this, avoid the dangers of adopting a patronizing tone, which might generate considerable resistance.

How can we progress from Class B to Class A in our negotiating tactics and style?

We can do this, first, by recognizing the temptations of Class B behaviours and then seeking Class A disciplines where these will be more appropriate and productive. If your organization constrains your behaviour, then either seek to change it through setting a better example or, if that fails, consider moving to a better/more professional environment elsewhere.

Build a reputation for your negotiating skills through a track record of significant success.

Preparing the case

We have seen that unprepared negotiators can be vulnerable to making mistakes; they may be skilled at covering them up but any serious errors will be discovered when the contract or agreement is implemented. In my previous book in this series, *Negotiation Skills In A Week*, we developed a thorough list-based approach to a case or project. This style has great strengths in 90 per cent of potential deals, as it lends itself to logical sequences, with positions, values and/or qualities that can be justified in the face of counter-proposals from an opponent. Rather more difficult are negotiations that involve:

- politics
- strategic choices
- long-term factors
- matters of principle
- 'what if?' issues.

Setting objectives and goals

A common preparation technique is using a grid that enables negotiating objectives to be identified and charted as follows:

Most favourable position ←------------→ Least favourable position

A principal benefit of this approach is that offers that lie outside the grid should, at least, trigger a review of your preparation and, on occasion, lead to the rejection of any deal that is not part of your team's aims.

Clearly, the more information that can be gained before the meeting the better; this should enable you to prepare a matrix that might give a clearer indication of where common ground might lie – and the scope for settlement. So, research is vital – for example collecting information from anyone else in your organization who might have some involvement with your intended partner. It is amazing how much of this kind of information can be gleaned. For example, you might get to hear of an internal instruction to line managers to clamp down on expenses claims because of a 'short-term cash-flow problem'. This might trigger an offer to include extended credit (or, indeed, the complete opposite).

A quality plan for negotiating a service contract could look like this:

Initial negotiating plan or grid

Our 'shopping list'	Negotiation objectives		Their 'shopping list'
Buyer e.g. price	US Most Favourable	US Least Favourable	**Vendor e.g. price**
	THEM Least Favourable	THEM Most Favourable	
	£72,000–£77,500	£72,500–£80,000	
Objective 2:	US MF	US LF	**Objective 2:**
e.g. delivery	THEM LF	THEM MF	**e.g. delivery**
	NOW!	6 months	
Objective 3:	US MF	US LF	**Objective 3:**
e.g. payment terms	THEM LF	THEM MF	**e.g. payment terms**
	3 months' credit	1 month	

> **TIP** *The challenge for quality standards in such a grid should focus on the following:*
>
> - **Precision:** *in being able to define a standard*
> - **Parameters:** *the need to establish parameters and priorities*
> - **Realism:** *not asking for the moon!*
> - **Aspirations:** *building in motivational targets to lift standards.*

Personal communication skills

One of the key fascinations with the task of negotiating is that success is dependent upon two vital functions: planning, then debating. The best results are achieved when attention is paid to both functions. Here is a reminder of the key skills that will repay the effort put into developing them over and over again:

- vocabulary
- speal/listen ratios
- comprehension
- non-verbal behaviour.

Vocabulary

Native English speakers are exceptionally fortunate that English is spoken in so much of the world. Like any language, the vocabulary is full of subtle nuances that convey different shades of meaning. For example, a negative situation can be expressed with a significant variation in strength, anywhere from 'a little local difficulty' to 'a complete disaster'. Either may be appropriate depending on the perception and mood of the speakers involved as well as the impact they would like to have on their fellow negotiator. There is an enormous power in the use of the right words when seeking to persuade your listeners – as all debaters understand!

However, those involved in the meeting must take care not to use an excess of technical vocabulary and jargon, as this may easily lead to confusion. Plain speaking should be the preferred style wherever possible.

Speak/listen ratios

Similarly, the best use of time in any meeting also needs careful consideration. A negotiation is unlikely to meet the true meaning of the word (or the aspiration needs of the participants) if one negotiator dominates most of the meeting time and speaks *at* the other party instead of talking *and* listening.

Maintaining the best balance will be affected by:

● the emotions involved
● the personal communication style of the people attending the meeting
● the seriousness of the issues
● the personality of each person attending
● the occupation of each person (salespeople, for example, are generally rather more extrovert than buyers).

Comprehension

Each of us has a variable speed at which our brain can comprehend what is being said – which is also affected by the speed of our opponent's communication style and language used. When we come to analyse the potential for misunderstandings, we need to recognize the potential for mistakes and exceptions – indeed, it is remarkable that more don't occur!

TIP *Concentrate hard on the content of what your opponent is saying, as well as the manner of its delivery. Never agree to anything that you do not fully understand – always seek clarification regarding WHO will do WHAT to WHOM and who will enforce this.*

Non-verbal behaviour

Behavioural scientists have developed frameworks on how to read the body language of others. The result is that we are more sensitive to signals sent by our opponents, whether they were intentional or not. Is this significant? Perhaps! A misread signal is potentially just as dangerous as one that was deliberately sent but ignored or missed.

A possible safety net may be provided where an additional observer attends your meeting who has the sole task of observing non-verbal signals sent during the meeting. Time would then be taken in a recess to feed back on any body language observed – together with an analysis of the possible meanings. A particularly fruitful use of this approach may be where the meeting includes a team of three or more people on your opponent's side.

Developing your personal negotiating style

Negotiating brings out very different reactions from people, sometimes leading them to put on an act (on the principle that emulating the style or behaviour of their favourite actor or entrepreneur is the best way of achieving top results). This is not a recommended strategy and certainly not one favoured by highly skilled negotiators.

However, a negotiation is usually dependent upon the exchange of information and some negotiators will seek to uncover as much as possible while attempting to reveal as little as possible. A healthy meeting is one in which relevant information is exchanged without any notion of 'gamesmanship' (which may risk the outcome agreement).

The processes in use in a meeting will be affected by two control issues:

1 Use of push/pull techniques

An example of this approach might involve one person trying to control the exchange of information by talking more or most of the time. This is rarely an effective control method. Better results are achieved through the use of controlling behaviours, which can be categorized into:

- Push
  - revealing facts/information
  - communicating feelings

- Pull
  - seeking answers to questions (especially open questions)
  - summarizing a discussion – encouraging agreement or revealing difficulties.

Push techniques tend to be used by salespeople, on the basis that sellers have to 'persuade actively' – otherwise, why would they exist? Pull techniques are traditionally used by purchasing people, who recognize potential problems that might occur if buying decisions were based simply on what salespeople want to declare. Critical factors may be those that the supplier would rather not answer. Of course, this example is an oversimplification, but the reader's use of control techniques in a negotiation may well affect the value of the outcome.

Behaviours to practise

Push		Pull
Giving information	INFORMATION	Seeking through questions
Speaking	PROPOSALS	Listening
	BUILDING IDEAS	
Offering ideas	EXPRESSING SUPPORT	Bringing in
	COUNTER-PROPOSAL	

Think before speaking

How you get your point across is as important, if not more so, than *what* you say because of the impact it may have upon others at the meeting.

Much as it may be interesting – and even entertaining – to work with 'high reactors', their extrovert nature can both create a barrier and generate exhaustion.

Top negotiators are skilled at:

- talking economically and purposefully
- listening attentively
- observing and analysing accurately
- speaking sensitively.

Sound preparation requires more than learning a script about needs or supplies; it also requires a commitment to, and understanding of, the strategy of our business and a personal determination to succeed with measurable outcomes.

Summary

SUNDAY

MONDAY

TUESDAY

WEDNESDAY

THURSDAY

FRIDAY

SATURDAY

This first day has reinforced the importance of:

● systematic, sensitive and accurate preparation *before* attending the meeting
● analysing the situation objectively
● thinking through the issues – those that are explicit, and
● seeking evidence to support those that are only implied.

In real life, most negotiators will claim that they do this. If/when their preparation turns out to be faulty or insufficient, they 'blag' it (while also claiming that this lack did not show or affect the outcome!). But haven't you noticed when your opponents have fallen into that trap?

Tomorrow, we will explore the issues that contribute to longer-term growth and success.

Now you have completed Sunday's chapter, complete the 'progress check' and then turn to the end of the book and make a commitment to your Personal Action Plan.

Progress check (answers at the back)

1. For best long-term results, negotiators should aim to achieve a deal that:
   a) Meets all objectives that satisfy their own organization ❑
   b) Meets their own 'shopping list' ❑
   c) Comes close to the objectives of both organizations ❑
   d) Meets all 'must achieve' objectives for both organizations ❑

2. It is good to achieve a reputation as a highly effective negotiator because:
   a) This will create an aura that will be off-putting for all other prospective negotiation partners ❑
   b) It will keep time-wasters at a distance ❑
   c) It is likely that most future deals will qualify as win/win arrangements ❑
   d) It is likely to bring early recognition and promotion ❑

3. Top negotiators:
   a) Talk more than they listen ❑
   b) Balance equally the time invested in preparation with time spent in debate ❑
   c) Use openly provocative statements to obtain top results ❑
   d) Are careful not to dominate by talking too much ❑

4. The 'pull' style is typically used by:
   a) Negotiators who have long experience in sales and marketing roles ❑
   b) Negotiators who think before they speak ❑
   c) Mainly negotiators who work in purchasing or procurement roles ❑
   d) Those negotiators who are really unsure of the case they are having to negotiate ❑

5. Misunderstandings in a negotiated agreement are a sign that:
   a) The deal will fail in the implementation stage ❑
   b) Insufficient preparation was carried out ❑
   c) One of the sides failed to clarify all the issues before reaching a deal ❑
   d) There could be genuine mistakes in the final record. ❑

6. For best long-term results, negotiators should aim to achieve a deal that:
   a) Meets all objectives that satisfy their own organization ❑
   b) Meets their own 'shopping list' ❑
   c) Comes close to the objectives of *both* organizations ❑
   d) Meets all 'must achieve' objectives for *both* organizations ❑

7. You have a client whose evident negotiating style is as a Naive/Introvert. Which style/tactics would be most appropriate for a productive and long-term relationship based on repeat business?

a) Adopt a Safety First role to avoid attracting blame if/when the proposals fail to meet their expectations ❑

b) Invest time to build up their trust and knowledge in your organization's expertise and proposals ❑

c) Build up trust by using the Completer-Finisher/Opportunist role ❑

d) Mirror their Naive/Introvert style to build their confidence ❑

8. Your new opponents' proposals already fit into the acceptable zone for most of your objectives. How would you respond?

a) Readily accept them – saving on time and energy ❑

b) Check all the finest detail to ensure there are no 'traps' ❑

c) Call a recess (e.g. coffee break) while you assess what could go wrong ❑

d) Build in progress checks to ensure that all commitments are fulfilled ❑

9. Your 'opponent' seems to 'tune out' in the conversation (with glazed eyes!). How would you respond?

a) Ask more questions – to test their concentration and understanding ❑

b) Suggest a recess or 'comfort break' in case they are experiencing a major distraction ❑

c) Introduce some new proposals to gain more interest ❑

d) Bring in a colleague to reinforce your impact ❑

10. You recently concluded a negotiation with a new 'opponent' and have already started to implement it as the deal is making a significant contribution to your objectives. However, you have now received their suggestion that it could be enhanced significantly and you fear that their interest is to recover their own 'lost ground' rather than help you. How would you respond?

a) Reject the suggestion outright, explaining that an urgent work commitment means that your time cannot be 'stretched' for another two months ❑

b) Request more written details before committing to any action ❑

c) Delegate the task to a colleague with strict instructions not to concede anything ❑

d) Agree a date as a priority as it will provide another opportunity to conclude another deal ❑

MONDAY

Negotiating growth through partnering

Most highly successful organizations owe their success to repeat business; a large element of this will have arisen from successful relationships with their partners (i.e. trusted suppliers, loyal clients and so on). Top negotiators are those who seek out such partnering opportunities and then build and develop them.

Today we will explore how to build a partnering relationship through:

- identifying best opportunities
- tuning in to partners' business culture and needs
- managing the challenges provided by project teams and specialists
- understanding how the the organization's stage of development can affect trust, behaviour and the use (or misuse) of power.

Whom should I seek as a partner?

Negotiators can face challenges in working out whom best to approach for their proposals. Is the first person we approach the right person to handle all subsequent contact? This chapter explores the basics of individual contact and also how your approach may need to change as the client organization and its way of handling key decisions develops. Understanding these processes is vital to a senior negotiator who is handling big contracts.

In simple terms, we need to be able to work with someone who has the freedom and authority to reach agreement – and then to see the fullest implementation of the agreement. That may sound simplistic but in reality it poses numerous challenges.

For example, a sales representative for a fashion house needs to identify and approach someone who is probably identified by a retail client as the fashion buyer. A door opens, an appointment is arranged and a presentation is made. However, it then transpires that the buyer is about to hand over responsibility for the budget to a new person who is yet to be appointed and therefore cannot commit that budget in the meantime. This is a frustrating situation, and one that should have been identified earlier.

At its simplest, ALL negotiators need to find the right people who have:

- *a recognition and knowledge of needs*
- *the necessary resources*
- *the time to meet*
- *the authority to negotiate*
- *the self-confidence to commit.*

Accessibility

Senior job titles are used to ascribe seniority (e.g. Buying Director, Credit Controller or Sales Manager) and from this we may be led to believe that the job holder has accountability for resources such as budgets, time and people. However, an additional commitment may not be in the budget and the board may have embargoed any additional spending in the current trading period. So, here are the key factors that need re-examination:

Authority and self-presentation

Interestingly, the nearer one gets to the top of an organization, the higher the risk of prevarication (or even reluctance to commit). This can be a painful lesson to learn – both inside and outside the chain of command – and may help to explain why seemingly simple issues are delayed while an internal negotiation has to take place to agree an appropriate way of handling the issue. So, job titles provide one route for communicating levels of authority, but this is not a foolproof rule.

Direct sales staff are taught that they should 'qualify the contact' – in other words, ensure that the person they are talking to fulfils the five criteria cited in the above tip. This is not easy, but it avoids investing a lot of time and effort in trying to influence people who simply do not have the authority to make the decision.

This dilemma may be eased by adding a Key Account Manager role into the normal hierarchy or by ensuring that directors are more accessible to support their sales teams when they have to negotiate issues that are outside their normal authority levels.

The next challenge is that business can only be transacted through people being accessible, authoritative and mindful of the need for persuasive self-presentation.

Organization to organization or person to person?

Email and texting make it far easier to communicate with business contacts and, because nowadays there are fewer personal secretaries who act as gatekeepers to their bosses' diaries, personal requests for interviews are more likely to be at least read, even if they are not always granted.

Looking at this process from the viewpoint of the 'target', is it really possible to manage in today's environment if you spend your life in an icebox? Accessibility is very important, even if it is for no other reason than to keep up with ever-changing possibilities and potential threats.

Towards a better understanding – the case for partnering

As organizations succeed and grow, so their market position changes. For example, the small local specialist may, quite quickly, become one that is multicultural and even multinational. With that growth comes greater challenge: an increased risk of competition both from existing competitors who need to defend their position in the marketplace, and also from other new entrants.

The risk of things going wrong also increases both because of the sheer scale of the operation or because of promises made that may not always be fulfilled. How the organization reacts in such situations can give a pretty clear indicator of the style with which it operates and – even more crucially – the way in which it exercises its power over weaker partners.

The **'power-over' complex** assumes that the other party's business exists only because 'our organization allows it' – an exaggeration that, in some instances, might be accurate.

A 'power-over' relationship may be domineering, even mean-spirited – especially when it comes to dealing with matters such as profit margins ('the more you make the less there is for me'). Good relationships in such a climate can quickly become competitive in the extreme, and may even lead to a complete relationship breakdown as alternatives are sought to break the 'power trap'.

The **'power-with' relationship,** on the other hand, assumes a more supportive partnership in which both parties aim for a genuine win/win outcome regarding matters such as shared profit margins, cost investment, market research and even technology development. Failures may still occur occasionally but they are dealt with in a non-punitive way, and parties seek to ensure that lessons are learned from the failure so that it does not recur.

Tune in to the business culture

Understanding the culture of your partner's business (and that of your own organization) can make a huge difference to the success of a negotiation and subsequent relationships:

Pioneers

The stage of development of your partner's organization may have less to do with size than state of play. In a sense, pioneers are easily recognized; their organization may be relatively new and their pioneering spirit can be witnessed at first hand.

Imagine this example: you wait in line for an interview with the MD of a company in the retail sector for, typically, half an hour before being granted a very short meeting – ten minutes or even less – punctuated by frequent telephone calls from suppliers and the MD barking out instructions. In such an environment it may be difficult, if not impossible, to develop a proposal for a longer-term case that may have a significant effect on the company's development.

The predominant negotiating style would appear to be one more commonly found in a street market and, unless something crucial changes, the same constraints are imposed on everyone.

The behaviour of pioneers can also be readily witnessed in their use of power over the people around them; this may not be pleasant to see (for example, if employees are publicly berated), but the picture conveys something of the reactions and punishment that may be exacted if someone fails to match expectations. Understanding that such an outcome is possible is as important as developing an approach that is time-economic and that conveys the key messages and potential benefits in an attractive and tempting way.

Remember, too, that the real power of pioneers might actually not lie within themselves; hidden behind them somewhere may be a family relative who exercises the real control and your normal contact is very reluctant to reveal this. This might explain lengthy periods of inaction, persuasion but no actual decision. In one case I know of, the 'frustrated persuader' learned about such constraints only from a chance discussion with another 'persuader'. 'The MD is not master of his own house,' he was told. 'The real power lies with his sisters who outvote him at every board meeting.' This piece of advice changed future negotiating strategy and more effort was put into persuasion strategies that the MD could use at board meetings.

Specialization

Once through the pioneer phase of business development (which in today's world may not take long), organizations tend to departmentalize their activities and authority levels. This can mean the freeing up of access and decision-making outside the bottleneck constraint of the pioneer. Setting up and operating budgetary controls is one obvious need, but another, more important, one is ensuring that key decisions on organization policy and commitment are followed by all players. This can lead to quite slow decision-making as access to the collective forum may still be controlled by the pioneer, who can use this political control to limit the freedom of colleagues to move the business forward.

Sharing responsibility through a group (typically a board of directors or management committee) ought to improve decision-making. However, if five-year plans, two- or three-year budget outlines, and an agreed trading policy do not exist, the new forum may not enjoy much effectiveness and, therefore, any opportunities for achieving agreement may still be restricted to the pioneer.

So, understanding how delegated authority is exercised is a vital point. Negotiations on everyday matters may be delegated, but a deal may become so large or so crucial to the future of the organization that a negotiator may need to adapt to a shift in the opponent's authority. For example, the negotiator could say that a particular issue needs to be dealt with by the board because of its potential impact on other divisions, which might be interpreted as 'I do not have the authority to negotiate that at the moment'.

A benefit here would be the learning possibilities derived from involvement with seniors, and gaining wider influence. A less positive aspect might be that the outcome could be considerably more time-consuming as meetings may be rather more dynamic, with more people involved and a mix of less predictable bargaining, management styles and objectives.

Integrated decision-making

As organizations grow and their structure becomes more complicated, decision-making may be conducted in 'committees'. High-performance organizations that are able to make this structure work have been known to avoid such distractions by adopting a different vocabulary – for example, a 'committee' may become a 'project team', 'sourcing team' or 'divisional board'. The presumption here is that the team shares authority and uses a more consultative management style before making properly costed recommendations.

TIP

Negotiating with project teams benefits from:

- *political sensitivity about the structure of the organization*
- *comprehensive briefing on a full scheme (not just a single purchase or sale)*
- *a persuasive approach for the verbal presentation (backed by a succinctly written paper)*
- *patience and sensitivity when dealing with questions/ key issues voiced by interested parties represented in the group*
- *personal belief in the scheme*
- *the ability to commit the time needed to develop full understanding and trust.*

Failing to arrive at a consensus in recommending a single forward decision or route (and thus incurring public criticism) can be an obvious hazard. Similarly, 'political' preferences may be allowed to supersede factual analysis. Such structures therefore require astute leadership from a trusted team leader who is also able to keep other power players in the organization informally briefed (an important ingredient in ensuring that a final recommendation does not come as a nasty surprise).

Organic structures

From time to time a negotiator may come across a more advanced organization structure where the client or supplier has a less usual way of incorporating individuals' skills into decision-making, even though the needs and benefits might seem to lie outside their own direct areas of responsibility. This approach is worth remembering when having informal discussions with people who appear to work in just one division of a business: their input, expertise and internal influence may extend well beyond their immediate 'paymasters'. As a consequence, potential suppliers of software might find themselves confronted with some very astute questioning in any sales presentation to the project team, and the credibility of the whole tendering process could be jeopardized by the way in which such discussions are managed and resolved.

Sensitive behaviours without which outcomes might be jeopardized include:

- *understanding organizational behaviour*
- *recognizing and impressing key influencers*
- *importance of maintaining confidentiality*
- *developing and maintaining 'partnership behaviours'.*

Power

No analysis of influence in negotiation would be complete without some reflection on the use (or misuse) of power. It can, of course, be reflective of the status of the individual, but in the majority of cases that individual power is delegated to us by an organization – which backs us. So, for example, an army officer has considerable authority over the soldiers in a particular division, but very little over the general population in peacetime (except, perhaps, in emergency situations). Negotiators need to understand the extent of an organization's power, as represented by a negotiator in whom trust may be placed to implement change. This is especially important when a new contract or agreement is likely to affect areas well outside the power and influence of your partner.

Individual v. organization power

A more in-depth analysis is impossible here, but influencers will benefit from comparing the following five characteristics:

1 **charismatic:** generally born of intellect, personality and self-presentation. This can be a power for good but overuse can lead to intimidation, which could be destructive.
2 **individual:** a person's career may be significantly affected by the outcomes of a case (both positively and negatively)
3 **manipulative:** for example, learned by children by the way they handle the comparative power of their parents. (Some employees use similar methods with their managers.)
4 **destructive:** especially when negotiations or the implementation of a deal fail
5 **organizational:** indicated by the job holder's power to inflict sanctions or provide 'bonuses' for good behaviour.

A case analysed

A sales opportunity could have a very different value if a company's market is found to be in decline. This shows that the value of partnering can also be affected by factors well outside the partner's control. The following table provides a distinctive comparison between the three organization phases that we have discussed:

	Pioneers	Specialization	Integrated
New proposals	Focus on quick returns	Demonstrate how a new idea helps expansion and reinforces 'difference'	Help achieve individuality and competitive advantage
Hiccups/ complaints	Speedy reaction; quick acceptance of ownership and corrective action	Corrective action and causes examined	Consequences of upset considered and factors affecting image addressed
Investment	Time for feedback	Specialist ideas – developing service/ product/functions	Reorganization of functions, e.g. vertical integration
Management information support	Reduce admin-istration time; help focus on support, how to overcome obstacles and barriers	Share own specialization and/ or knowledge to support one other in a non-competitive way	Focus effort on achieving the results that contribute to the 'big picture'
Promises	Always readily fulfilled and action communicated	Shown importance by actions and words	Delegated but followed up and communicated

In the end, the successful negotiator seeks to build, develop, and maintain a trusting relationship with long-term business partners. This is easily stated but all too easily destroyed with just one careless decision in the organization. For example, if the main point of contact in an organization moves into a new role and their replacement fails to provide the same level of care, then previous organizational influence will begin to wane.

Seniority: effectiveness v. trust

You might think that the best practices listed in the above panel are the normal mark of most senior executives in any organization and that more junior negotiators need to be sharper in order to meet short-term objectives. Wrong!

If we were to substitute 'more economical with the truth' for 'sharper', some negotiators might decide that partnering is too expensive and that 'influential presentation' is all that is really necessary: 'Tell them what they want to hear, back it up with early action and the next events will take care of themselves!'

Wrong again! It is the actions that matter; talking a good game is not enough. Surely there is little point in occupying an influential position unless it provides the opportunity to create change and ensure that it is fulfilled as originally envisaged. Here lies the origin of the expression 'My word is my bond'. Sadly, there have been infamous incidences on the public stage where this expression has definitely not applied to either the outcome or the operational methods involved. Would we want to build a business relationship over years with such a person who has broken trust and clearly not worried about it?

Continuity and behaviour

What if all these expectations seem to be unrealistic? Behaving politely to someone who demonstrates little concern for politeness or manners themselves can be difficult. A lack of manners may be a sign of a lack of interest in the other party's needs, although it may not necessarily indicate that the negotiator is engaging in 'sharp practice' or is being economical with the truth. In this case, you may need to bring a slower pace to a negotiation and take care not to make speedy deals, since trust has not yet been established.

Care should be taken with assumptions made about new 'opponents', a little prior research could prove invaluable.

Thorough ice-breaking in early meetings helps to build new relationships; there is a vital difference between making a quick sale or purchase and building a longer-term, more trusting relationship.

Resisting the misuse of power

How easy is it to cope with uncomfortable situations that may arise from the misuse of power? In the short term, it may be necessary for a negotiator to grin and bear it on the basis that the concluded negotiations and results delivered are what will earn respect from the other person or organization. However, this does not mean giving in to unreasonable requests or acquiescing to unwarranted bullying tactics. Clear boundaries need to be drawn and defended. Consider the following dialogue:

Client: I would not be able to do business on these terms. Everyone else we work with is offering us 60 days' free credit and accepting full responsibility for advertising us as a stockist. If you cannot match that, I'm afraid we would find it extremely difficult to do business this time.

Possible response: I understand your point. We too could offer similar terms, but they would be entirely dependent upon the level of business that we are able to do together. The more business you place, the better the terms could be.

This kind of response is really saying: 'We want to do business with you and I understand that you would prefer better terms than quoted. If you are able to clarify what you'd like to buy, then I promise to give you a better insight into how we could help you.' A more explicit response could have led to bargaining over discount rates and declaring a position when there was actually no clear or firm indication that the client wanted to do business at all.

TIP *Negotiation is about uncovering knowledge and information before trading something for something. Giving away information – and gaining little or nothing in return – leads to poor deals and encourages bullying tactics from opponents.*

Summary

Whether they recognize it or not, all organizations need help and support. Negotiators often have opportunities for providing ideas and independent feedback that can be very valuable to their opponents, especially when their track record has shown that they can be fully trusted (and that their suggestions are not just recommendations of self-interest). Senior negotiators must have a good understanding about authority and power and how decisions can be influenced with proven ideas gained from experiences elsewhere. Such relationships underpin long-term partnering that can have a huge impact on business results for both organizations.

Now that you have completed Monday's study, complete the 'progress check' and then turn to the end of the book and make a commitment to your Personal Action Plan.

SUNDAY

MONDAY

TUESDAY

WEDNESDAY

THURSDAY

FRIDAY

SATURDAY

Progress check (answers at the back)

1. As well as achieving measurable results, negotiators should always try to be in control of:
   a) Meeting all objectives that satisfy their own organization ❏
   b) The location of the meeting ❏
   c) Their opponents' strategies ❏
   d) Their own destiny ❏

2. 'Qualifying' your opponent means:
   a) Checking that your opponent has the right qualifications for the job in hand ❏
   b) Being a Completer/Finisher ❏
   c) Ensuring that you are negotiating with someone at the right level for the deal to be implemented successfully ❏
   d) Building a strong relationship with the most senior person available ❏

3. 'Partnering' means:
   a) Exerting power over your contact and their organization ❏
   b) Meeting all the expectations of your boss and the seniors on the other side ❏
   c) Building and maintaining a sharing relationship with your partner organization ❏
   d) Ensuring frequent meetings – even social ones over a coffee ❏

4. Understanding the stage of development of your partner's organization is:
   a) Helpful as it helps achieve much higher results ❏
   b) About understanding the history of the organization and how it achieved its current state ❏
   c) Useful for gaining a better opportunity to maintain influence as a trusted supplier ❏
   d) Helpful for reaching a better understanding of how power is used ❏

5. Playing politics inside the client organization by taking sides and/or promoting one person's interests is:
   a) Understandable, as senior executives often need impartial advice ❏
   b) A matter of how authority is delegated in the organization ❏
   c) Dangerous and should be avoided at all costs ❏
   d) A matter of maintaining a balance between common sense and looking after your own organization's interests ❏

6. When bringing a project team together it is best to:
a) Maintain its membership within the user department to ensure credibility with users ❑
b) Bring together representatives with expertise from a wide range of interests in the organization ❑
c) Ensure that adequate time is made available – both as lead time and as a resource ❑
d) Leave political grandstanding outside the door ❑

7. Power in a project team needs to be carefully balanced if creative as well as practical ideas are to be developed. This is the task of:
a) The project leader who needs authority and leadership skills to manage the team ❑
b) Each member, although they should not overstep their role ❑
c) The person who established the team in the first place ❑
d) The organization's management team ❑

8. Depending on how a pioneer organization is developing, partnering by negotiators provides opportunities for the organization to benefit from:
a) Quick results from proposals (with minimal time investment) ❑
b) Upsets, which need to be handled sensitively ❑
c) Complaints, especially those whose origins cannot be easily identified ❑
d) Delegation ❑

9. Ensuring that agreements are implemented is best achieved by the most senior person available. This means:
a) Negotiators should ignore the efforts of more junior people in a client organization ❑
b) Negotiators should try to match their own seniority in their own organization with their normal contact with their partnered organizations ❑
c) Trust is built up by implementation and actions, not words (or rank!) ❑
d) We can believe what we want to believe when being briefed by the project's senior executive ❑

10. The achievement of longer-term partnerships for all negotiators in all situations is:
a) A luxury that most negotiators have insufficient time to implement ❑
b) Dependent entirely upon the situation and importance to the negotiator's organization ❑
c) A good starting point, enabling negotiators to develop their partnering skills ❑
d) A worthy ideal that would be unnecessary in many day-to-day situations ❑

TUESDAY

Effective influence in negotiation

So far we have looked at negotiating during the early stages of building a relationship. Obviously, the longer negotiators have worked together the more likely it is that they have an understanding about each other's style, methods and preferred ways of working. Also, crucially, past arrangements that were agreed will have been opened up to scrutiny and all parties will have a view on how successful they proved to be in reality. At its simplest, this means that negotiators will know who did what to whom, how it worked out, and whether they want to do it again if the opportunity arose.

It is entirely reasonable for past experiences to resurface in later meetings, which is a good reason for ensuring that any disputes are resolved whenever they occur. If ill-feeling is allowed to persist, it could have a negative effect on the next deal and make it much harder to maintain a constructive atmosphere.

Today's topic – effective influence – can be defined as how easily we can persuade other people to accept our proposals. We will also introduce an overall framework for meetings – as used by high-performing negotiators – which helps ensure a businesslike approach and that our goals are addressed much more efficiently.

PROD-ProSC – a development framework

Negotiating skills can be more readily developed if a systematic approach is applied. This is not to say that meetings cannot be unstructured or conducted in a very informal way. However, the risk with this style is that one party – or even both – forgets to raise issues or close them off; once the meeting is over, any attempt to reopen the negotiation can feel like a potential trick. In any case, there is no point setting up a meeting and then having to call another one a few days later to renegotiate something that it was thought had been agreed in the first place. Hardly the mark of a well-managed process! And the key aim is to ensure that both sides can arrive at an agreement that they both *want* to implement.

Consider the following framework for effective negotiations:

P - Preparation

R - Research (when needed)

O - Open the meeting

D - Discussion

Pro - Proposals

S - Summarize

C - Close

Creating influential impressions

This book assumes that the reader already has considerable experience in building a good rapport with other negotiators. Suffice to say that an open relationship based on good manners (and a little charm) will help to keep the wheels of the negotiation oiled. All the relevant points about showing respect for one other through self-presentation are important – this is especially true of the way we dress, speak and display general courtesy and manners.

However, the best starting point is being able to reflect on past deals that have been successfully implemented and, where they have not, being able to agree a suitable action plan to put matters right. New business can now be developed, with lessons learned, so that any past errors will not recur.

SUNDAY MONDAY TUESDAY WEDNESDAY THURSDAY FRIDAY SATURDAY

> **TIP** *People are rarely prepared to talk about the future when they are still smarting from past failures or disappointments!*

All this assumes that, in continuing relationships, the negotiators concerned have already communicated past performance problems so that appropriate action can be taken. Unfortunately, some people (who see life as one long power game) may be tempted to use such events as an opportunity for an unexpected and sudden attack (with the aim of putting their opponent on the back foot), in the expectation that this will wring more generous compensation or allowances. Playing such games rarely creates positive relationships and can easily generate sufficient ill-feeling for opponents to adopt similar tactics. Such an approach, then, may well prove counterproductive.

The starting point

The perfect impression to make is one where the host has managed the environment so that there are:

- no unexpected interruptions
- a confidential atmosphere
- witnesses/assistants who are properly briefed and introduced
- technological samples or displays that work perfectly
- ready access to past records or paperwork that may be needed.

Clearly, in such a meeting there will also be the expectation that all participants are up to date with all the necessary reading and understand what is involved. This especially applies to agenda if this has been drafted and shared in advance.

Subtle ways of leading the meeting

High-performing negotiators use specific behavioural techniques that, while they can be used by both sides to good effect, do not, on their own, normally lead to a negative reaction from the opposition. What most negotiators seek is an outcome that meets their aims and objectives – and this also applies to our opponents. Achieving a win/win situation is not about gaining the upper hand but arriving at the point where both sides want to be committed to the deal.

Influence and personality

Can you think of someone you know – perhaps someone you have worked with – whom you find yourself almost always agreeing with? This could be something to do with that person's charismatic personality. Or perhaps they display all the qualities that you think should be found in an ideal manager, contractor, counsellor, teacher or client.

Do you find that you look forward to discussions with them because, whatever the subject, you know that you will not find it difficult to find common ground and reach an agreement? Some of the traits that contribute to an agreeable personality are innate, but good conversation skills can also be developed.

The negative effects of poor conversations skills cannot be underestimated. A negotiator may be self-centred, almost boasting about past or current deals achieved and demonstrating that they are 'top dog'. This might have a distinctly off-putting effect on some people. Equally irritating can be the person who quizzes you about all that you have done, are doing, or hope to achieve while never revealing their own experiences. Both can be conversational tactics designed to gain an upper hand in the relationship.

Good conversationalists and negotiators balance the give-and-take as it takes time to reach an understanding of how a good relationship can be formed (unless, of course the deal is a one-off arrangement and the two parties will never meet again). Take greater care in this situation as many win/lose tricks may be used. We do not have space to cover these in this book, which concentrates on the collaborative bargaining that is normally a feature of long-term relationships.

Behaviours used by highly effective negotiators

Here are some key elements that are worth polishing for future meetings:

Leadership and control in discussion

This does not mean doing all the talking or ensuring that your ideas dominate the discussion and in the final record of the negotiation. Leadership and control come from ensuring that concepts and opinions are shared and this is less likely to happen if one party is too forceful, dogmatic or domineering, effectively monopolizing the discussion. Natural-born leaders with magnetic personalities are, however, the exception to this rule. Although they are not common, if you think you might fall into this category you are very lucky and you may be able to short-cut many negotiations simply by using your natural charisma!

Persuasive outcomes are more likely to be achieved by adopting the following behaviours:

- **Seeking information:** especially by the use of open questions – that is, those that begin with *who?*, *what?*, *when?*, *where? why?* or *how?* These draw information from the opponent and help ensure that all vital details are covered before a deal is decided.
- **Proposing:** this is a vital behaviour as proposals are really the only way of moving a negotiation forward. Ideas are usually too vague to achieve much on their own. However, introducing a trial proposal, phrased something like 'Suppose we were able to...' gives the impression that this is just an idea that could be firmed up into a formal proposal if both sides agree.
- **Testing understanding:** use phrases such as 'Can I just clarify a point here?' or 'Let's just make sure we all understand your idea', followed by a restatement by either

party, or a direct question such as 'What exactly did you mean by...?' or 'How would you see that arrangement working in practice?'

● **Supporting:** this is valuable because offering support for another party's ideas encourages them to listen better to the ways in which you feel the proposal can be enhanced. Nothing is guaranteed to demotivate people more than the rubbishing of their ideas, and there may be serious negative outcomes if you give the impression that your ideas are the only ones that count and any others are worthless. A good way of showing support for others' ideas might be: 'I like the approach you have suggested and would like to discuss it in more detail, especially the costs and how to make it work in practice.' Note that expressing support for an idea does not mean that you have committed to act upon it, only that you would be happy to see it feature in the overall agreement, if possible.

● **Building:** this is another way of expressing support, but this time the other party's ideas are added to by offering an additional/linked idea or proposal that enhances the original idea and makes it even more attractive (either to you or, preferably, to both sides). This approach also provides an alternative to direct and explicit disagreement or using a potentially provocative counter-proposal.

● **Summarizing:** this is a very useful tactic as it gives all parties a second chance to ensure that they have heard any proposals and that they understand these proposals and (preferably) agree with them. Summaries are often signalled with the word 'So...'.

● **Reflecting feelings:** sharing inner thoughts, while not always a feature of negotiators' chosen style of communication, can be a very powerful way of gaining movement or advantage in discussion. The reasoning behind this is that no one can claim that you do *not* feel unsure, uneasy or unhappy (or even excited, pleased or confident) and these feelings are either an encouraging sign or a potential barrier to agreement. An example could be: 'I am feeling a little unsure about this approach to our problem and would like to take some advice about it before proceeding.'

These approaches may seem familiar to the reader – what might be new is that they are being presented as powerful conversational tactics that can apply in many different circumstances. However, their use can make achieving positive results in a negotiation much easier and they can bring a lasting benefit in that opponents feel more comfortable about the persuasion and influence that have been applied.

Negative behaviours

If this all sounds like an idealized situation where negotiators are always on their best behaviour, the following list will provide behaviours that are best kept under control, since they tend to work against achieving an agreement:

- **Counter-proposals:** if haggling goes on for too long in a meeting, it can become tiresome. It can inject a feeling of competition into the meeting and is best avoided in serious business negotiations where the intention is to arrive at a win/win collaborative agreement.
- **Shutting out:** this is a very frustrating behaviour in which one person endeavours to talk over another with the aim of gaining their submission to the ideas or information presented. In the Western world this borders on bad manners and is therefore best avoided, since it may generate another barrier to reaching agreement. In other parts of the world it may be culturally acceptable but still should not be resorted to as a frequent tactic.
- **Disagreeing:** negotiations do often include disagreements but skilled negotiators are more likely to provide a reasoned statement rather than a plain 'I disagree with you there', which is unlikely to help move the discussion along. A good negotiator will also label the disagreement before it is stated, which encourages the listener to concentrate on the reasons behind the disagreement before reacting.
- **Blocking:** this tactic places an obstacle in the way of the discussion and is designed to prevent progress. A typical statement might be 'We could never agree with that!', with no reason provided, or 'That's not even as good as the

offers currently available from your competitors!' Frequent blocking creates frustration, and frustration can lead to a walkout.

- **Defence/attack:** when all else fails, negotiators have been known to attack their opponents verbally. This might provide a useful means of exhausting their frustration or anger but it is also likely to have unwanted consequences and may well lead to a loss of control on either side. Conflicts are best resolved through reasoned argument. Some people, however, believe that this will come about only after the conflict has been exhausted. An example of this is the peace talks that may follow bitter industrial disputes between management and trade unions.

- **Argument dilution:** this means presenting every single argument in support of your own proposal, only some of which are strong ones. When these have been listed, your opponent only has to wait for you to stop speaking and then they can reverse the process by destroying each argument in turn, from the weakest to the strongest. By the time the strongest argument has been reached you may not be quite so convinced as you were that you have a sound case. This is an example of where quantity is less powerful than quality when it comes to making your argument.

Remember that skilled negotiators work hard to avoid using these behaviours – even to the point of taking a low-key, placid role in the meeting: 'If I cannot find something positive to say, then I'd prefer not to say anything that might make matters worse.'

Of course, by their very nature meetings tend to feature a considerable amount of conversation, which may or may not have a distinct bearing on the case being discussed. Any meeting will be made easier if there is a little small talk before the parties get down to business. This should give some invaluable clues as to the prevailing mood of the parties present. From the perspective of the case under discussion, however, the behaviours used in any meeting are most likely to have a neutral effect on the negotiation, unless one party is tempted to use a conversational red herring and introduce a topic that is really a distraction or a piece of misinformation. Once again, this form of gamesmanship can easily backfire and is best avoided.

Neutral behaviours

Not everything that is shared in the meeting will be readily categorized into having 'good' or 'bad' effects. Consider the following behaviours, some of which you may have witnessed in the course of negotiations:

- **Giving information:** it might be surprising that this behaviour is labelled as 'neutral'. It is defined as such because too much information can overcomplicate or cause confusion. You may have encountered someone whose excessive readiness to chat and share in-depth detail can be extremely wearing. As a consequence, the listener may become less willing to reach a ready agreement, unless it is out of desperation to close the meeting! If the presenter's style is also to bring an excess of obscure technical language to the discussion, the meeting may end up in a 'fog' from which it will become impossible to reach a clear agreement.

- **Talking:** it is highly possible to talk a lot and actually not say a great deal. Equally, if you are a 'low reactor' – or prefer not to talk very much – your opponent may struggle to know how to handle the meeting. They might:
  - babble, that is talk for the sake of filling the silence
  - make lots of proposals, each one better than the last
  - create a 'sob story', seeking your sympathy in order to agree a deal
  - reveal information that actually gives you reasons why you should *not* do business together.

If you have found yourself doing any of these things, then try instead to focus on listening. Using the open questions previously discussed will help you to become a better conversationalist and, hence, negotiator. When we are proposing to do business together, the resulting deal may be intended to be a long-term one; it would be far better to make sure that that relationship is based on shared facts and open information that will help to develop trust between the parties.

Strategy and team building

On our side

Negotiation is important in many everyday relations between people who are interdependent. This may be seen in families, between neighbours, and when we are engaged in everyday interactions such as shopping. These provide good opportunities for team building so that home-based discussions can serve as a model for negotiating agreements outside the home. It can be very difficult to reach agreement with a group of people when there are no constraints in place on the methods to be used (for example, one member may much prefer to attack when another much prefers logical argument); but the most important tool is to be prepared to compromise. Cynics claim that a compromise means that no one achieves what they really want, but a worse outcome would be to end up with no positive result whatsoever after hours of discussion.

Across the divide

Teamworking skills across the supplier/client divide are discussed rather less frequently; this might be because convention dictates that confidences need to be maintained, for example regarding vital elements such as operational costs and profit margins. Much damage to team relationships can result when employees are tempted to share more information with suppliers or customers than they should. It may be tempting to divulge information to opponents if you feel that you have developed a more personal relationship with them, especially if they seem to be more friendly than employees in your own organization.

TIP *A clear strategy with precise rules on inter-organizational data is vital if confidences are to be shared but not misused within the 'family'.*

Why team negotiation?

Some people think that a stronger case can be made by preparing a large team to support the main negotiator at crucial meetings. Certainly, a well-chosen team – who have been thoroughly briefed on their individual and team roles – can be a valuable source of influence in a meeting. However, the reverse is also true and an overly large team with little understanding of order and strategy may risk bringing the meeting to a chaotic end. Hand-picking the delegates needed for a team is important, but so too is ensuring that they are briefed in detail, including guidelines on desirable forms of behaviour to be practised.

Behaviour in negotiating teams

Ideally, a team should comprise no more than three or four people. Sometimes, however, circumstances dictate that it has to be larger, perhaps because of the expertise needed or the representational roles of those attending. The most powerful use of team members lies in casting them into specific roles, which might include:

● leader (and deputy)
● secretary/note-taker
● specialists, such as a finance specialist, a planning officer or an HR adviser
● observers of the opposing team.

For such a team, a plan is needed to manage intra-team communications, for example by passing notes during negotiating sessions (and during recesses if and when they are called). Authority for implementing all of this should rest with the team leader whose task is to consult team members, allocate roles, and orchestrate team presenters as seems appropriate during each session.

A team manifesto

It is easy to prepare such a list in the peace of a quiet office, but the value of an overall plan (albeit a flexible one) will be seen as it should guide discussion and action in the meeting itself. There is always the risk, of course, that if both sides prepare a fixed plan the first negotiation is likely to be about whose plan will be adopted! Leading a team includes ensuring that all members pull together and this may require a thorough briefing: a team manifesto is a good place to start.

Sample team manifesto

Here is our checklist of 12 key points: We aim to:

1 apply a give-and-take approach, that is seek to exchange something for something
2 use the truth in our descriptions, avoiding claims when we know that they are in dispute or positively untrue
3 take care over arranging the meeting; if we are hosting, we should book a quiet room, ensure that there will be no interruptions, and make sure that visitors and hosts alike are comfortable
4 agree a strategy within our team, including rules regarding who talks and when (avoiding 'multi-speak' and shutting others out by talking over them)
5 agree how the team will be led and by whom – and actively defend that role
6 support the leader's control over the processes involved
7 try to be open-minded to new ideas, which may achieve our desired results but by a different route
8 listen courteously and always speak politely
9 be sensitive to time and timing and encourage the other side to believe that any agreement is their own free commitment, regardless of any power issues

> 10 provide the opportunity for intra-team confidential consultation in a secure place, as no intra-team disagreements should be voiced in the meeting
>
> 11 accept any deficiencies in performance, apologizing as necessary but stopping short of offering compensation unless this is part of a wider agreement to remove any threat of possible legal action
>
> 12 resist all temptation to engage in defence/attack spirals, unless the leader gives specific approval.

Rules of engagement

Leaders should also establish rules of engagement. These might include:

- No unplanned inputs are to be made (by anyone!) without the leader's request and approval.
- All discussion on strategy and progress is to take place in recesses which the leader will call if and when necessary.
- During negotiating sessions, communication within the team should be carried out by passing notes.
- The hosting team will ensure that both teams have access to a private and confidential side room to be used for preparation and recesses. (It goes without saying that these need to be secure or the credibility and trust of either party may be compromised.)

Recesses provide valuable opportunities to:

- consider what progress has been made to date against the original objectives
- revise objectives if necessary, especially taking account of proposals received from the other team
- reconsider planned concessions and how they might be exchanged to achieve movement from the opposing team
- regroup the team if necessary (for example, if anyone's attention is wandering)
- obtain feedback from team observers and specialists (particularly on the non-verbal signals being used in the

opposing team, such as eye contact, and also any hints about intra-team communication).

It should always be remembered that the larger the meeting, the greater the risk of discussions descending into chaos, through which all involved can lose credibility. This is an argument for keeping away from team negotiations wherever and whenever possible. The method is certainly not a panacea for all problems.

Given the potential for things to go wrong, all who are likely to be involved in a team negotiation should attend specialized practical training in order to avoid outcomes becoming chaotic. Especially to be avoided are insufficient listening and thinking before speaking. A lack of self-discipline can have a terminal effect on anything constructive being achieved.

Summary

Two main advantages can be gained from the systematic approach to negotiating meetings described today:

1 The framework helps ensure that the meeting is complete and that neither party feels it necessary to reopen the discussion days after the meeting because something was missed out.

2 Once the behaviour analysis method described becomes second nature, greater clarity and control over progress towards a mutually acceptable agreement will result.

These benefits will mean that any tension in meetings is reduced and mutual respect is enhanced. Further, the approach can be applied by everyone involved (especially in team negotiations) and thus emotional or unstructured behaviours – which can provide major distractions – reduced or eliminated.

Now you have completed Tuesday's study, complete the 'progress check' and then turn to the end of the book and make a commitment to your Personal Action Plan.

SUNDAY

MONDAY

TUESDAY

WEDNESDAY

THURSDAY

FRIDAY

SATURDAY

Progress check (answers at the back)

1. The PROD-ProSC framework is:
a) Only a guide and should not be used as a 'straitjacket' for each and every negotiation ☐
b) Useful for keeping the meeting on track ☐
c) Useful for new negotiators when considering their preparations ☐
d) A valuable planning aid, especially for high-profile or high-risk negotiations ☐

2. A major obstacle for reaching a new agreement is:
a) One of the participants behaving in a provocative manner ☐
b) Being late for the meeting or appointment ☐
c) Either side failing to agree on a suitable course of action ☐
d) Having outstanding issues or failures from earlier negotiations still on the table ☐

3. Oiling the wheels of a negotiation is best achieved by:
a) Ensuring that regular supplies of drinks and other refreshments are available ☐
b) Having an additional room available for confidential recesses ☐
c) Good manners... and maybe a little charm ☐
d) Clarity in communication – both written and verbal ☐

4. 'Neutral' behaviour in a negotiation is:
a) A criticism of the other side ☐
b) Behaviour that achieves very little in terms of progressing the negotiation ☐
c) A compliment ☐
d) A proposal ☐

5. Negotiating in a team requires:
a) Self-control and discipline, thereby minimizing the risk of 'multi-speak' ☐
b) A sense of mission and self-belief ☐
c) Defence/attack if and when necessary ☐
d) Maintaining loyalty to the team and its objectives ☐

6. Seeking advice in a negotiation should invite
a) An attack for wasting time ☐
b) A summary of progress to date ☐
c) The suggestion of a recess ☐
d) The offer of clarification from your opponents ☐

7. You can never provide too many summaries in a negotiation because:
a) Summaries help to clarify all that has been said or agreed so far ☐
b) They give everyone the opportunity to concentrate on what to say next ☐
c) They take the heat off the lead negotiator ☐
d) They help to use up the time ☐

8. A lot of counter-proposing is:
a) A sign of a win/lose culture between negotiators ❑
b) A risk that could lead to defence/attack cycles ❑
c) A hint that agreement will be impossible ❑
d) An indicator of a very competitive negotiator ❑

9. Giving multiple reasons for an argument or proposal:
a) Weakens the proposal as it gives opponents more grounds on which to attack ❑
b) Encourages critics to think that the team is over-eager ❑
c) Strengthens the case because of the increased number of supporting reasons provided ❑
d) Distracts the team from the key behaviours that are needed ❑

10. A team manifesto is designed to:
a) Bring team members together so that they are committed to their strategy ❑
b) Show opponents that the team means business ❑
c) Enable team members to work towards a common goal ❑
d) Avoid misunderstandings occurring in the negotiation meeting ❑

WEDNESDAY

Making proposals and trading concessions

For all the benefits gained from our early discussions this week, readers will quickly recognize that productive negotiating will not happen unless the strategic preparation and self-presentation are matched by the ability to manage the potential cut-and-thrust of the actual conversation.

Today we will learn how to make forward progress in the conversation – that is, how best to:

- use proposals
- deal with counter-proposals
- avoid stalemate
- maintain influence
- negotiate in teams and avoid common mistakes, especially when emotions are running high!

Proposals

There are two types of proposal: process proposals and content proposals. Recognizing and consciously using the different applications provides additional practice for both parties (i.e. in talking and listening).

Process proposals

At its simplest, the sentence 'Let's make a start' represents a proposal that begins the process of getting the task started. Even though this is presumably what the parties have come together to do, most of us would prefer to break the ice with some small talk, which has several purposes:

● to weigh up the opposition and find out more about their style and attitudes
● to give the participants a chance to relax, as they may be in a strange place
● to ensure a seamless process from previous correspondence and/or telephone contact, and thus avoid any possible misunderstandings from those starting points.

Content proposals

In a negotiation, the only type of behaviour that will make forward progress is a content proposal. Many negotiators are reluctant to make proposals too early in a meeting as they are worried about pitching too high or too low. If a written specification has already been submitted – together with a quotation – this has to be the best starting point and should be defended – otherwise, why was it submitted at this value in the first place?

From either side, there may be some factors that could help in simplifying the complications and costing of the assignment, which could in turn bring about some changes. Alternatively, it may be that the contractor has a timetable where a new contract could fit into a precise calendar period when there would otherwise be a downturn in work schedules.

Therefore, it is most likely that both sides will have included some wriggle room over the specification and this will provide scope for change in the proposal. This might be expressed in the form of enhanced supply (higher value at the quoted price, or a concessionary price at the same specification, or something at a lower specification).

So, the well-recognized formula 'If you can do *this* for us, then we could do *that* for you' can lead to a series of exchanges until the two sides feel that they are in balance and ready to close. This simplified approach should help to remove some of the mystique and pressure. We shall now explore some of the related skills involved.

Seeking movement: proposals revisited

As we have seen, many people have a dilemma: they don't want to demand the earth but equally don't want to be offered very little. The risk is that a proposal that is too low (or too generous) will be immediately accepted by the opposition who see a quick and cheap way of overcoming a small problem before it becomes widely known – and therefore more costly!

Success from enhanced concepts

Successful negotiations require some action by two people or organizations. For example, 'If you'll agree to take up the old flooring and dispose of it, then we'll agree to fit the new carpet for nothing' – in other words, action on one side is dependent on action on the other. An important improvement point would be to work on improving the balance of cost or value between concessions granted versus those gained. Are you over-generous with concessions granted, perhaps because of a fear that no agreement will be reached? If this is the case, what further research could you undertake to clarify current market values?

The pressure to agree

What are the consequences of a failure to agree? One party feels that the cost/benefit debated is not commensurate with the facilities, services or actions that are offered. It may also mean that both sides are unhappy, in which case the result could be an outright failure to agree. We would consider this situation to be a stalemate or, in simpler language, a lose/lose.

In reality, the loss might be minimal – perhaps only the investment of time – although, if one party had travelled on a plane to a different continent, then the loss would feel real and potentially very costly! Such time investment can also become a pressure point to force concessions to reach an agreement. In one case I know of, the supplier was in Cambodia and, quite unmercifully, used this remote location to put pressure on a visiting client to raise his offer or go home empty-handed. It worked, of course.

The only problem with this kind of strategy is that the client might never want to do business with that company again. However, if your company is confident that it has the best product, guaranteed to be available on time and in full, and clients are queuing up to purchase, then perhaps it is a chance worth taking. Are you faint-hearted when it comes to rejecting others' proposals? Would you like to say, 'Where did that idea come from? There's no way I could ever agree to that!', but are afraid that their response might be 'Goodbye, then!'? Could you practise expressing disagreement more positively without closing the door on discussions?

Draft a positive version – one that still gives you control of the outcome.

Trial proposals can help

In less pressurized climates, negotiators may not feel like making positive proposals too early, instead preferring to pause and tease out reactions to a possible proposal. In such a situation, trial proposals are a useful way to make progress without risking a win/lose outcome.

Try the following examples:

- 'I suppose we might be able to improve the offer... How could you help?'
- 'How about we cancel this account and start afresh?'

In each case there is a clear signal: here is an idea that might move things along and, if it is acceptable, we could make it part of our overall agreement. Clearly, like any proposal, this idea has the potential to be extended or improved.

TIP *The way in which a proposal is received usually signals whether further discussion is likely to be fruitful, totally rejected, or somewhere in between.*

Counter-proposals

A distinguishing mark of highly competitive negotiators lies in their use of counter-proposals. A simple example would be where one negotiator proposes £10 as the preferred price in a contract and the opponent (with barely a pause) responds that £8 is better. So the bidding continues until agreement – or a sticking point – is reached.

Why is all this significant? Culturally, in Europe (especially the UK) the preference is for negotiators to use a collaborative style rather than a more aggressive, competitive style. This is borne out by extensive research and contrasts markedly with the convention in other parts of the world. For example, a more competitive style can be witnessed in the United States. However, it should be remembered that we are contrasting different cultural conventions, not just those of nationality. This means that a European who works for – or has been trained by – an American-based organization is more likely to favour, and use, the more explicit and sharper competitive style.

TIP *Counter-proposals tend to be much less used by collaborative negotiators than by competitive negotiators. In a typical one-hour meeting a collaborative negotiator is likely to use only one or two counter-proposals. Habitual competitive negotiators would find this figure very low.*

This difference in negotiating style extends even further: if the thrust and counter-thrust is not resolved quickly, then exchanges can migrate very quickly into defence/attack. Once that happens, everything has the potential to spiral out of control. All this may occur with little warning – especially if the subject matter for the negotiation is already emotive – and there may be a need to exhaust these emotions before serious bargaining can take place. It may be helpful to engage the services of a conciliator, whose contribution would be to clarify the issues before encouraging the adversaries to move towards each other. Clarification may also involve exposing the inner feelings that have built up through a frustrating period of proposing and counter-proposing.

Exposing inner feelings is a very powerful tactic even in a collaborative meeting; this is mainly because no one can disagree with the existence of another person's inner feelings.

Highly skilled negotiators are able to bring both competitive and collaborative negotiators to agreement by adjusting their style to meet the challenge.

Avoiding stalemate: be creative to avoid a lose/lose situation

When both sides have moved but are still not in a concluding position, we might describe this as a potential stalemate. Here are some alternative actions:

- Trade off movement on this deal with an allowance or concession made regarding another current deal between the same parties.
- Adjust the issues with a very small concession (after a token debate) that accepts the principle but at very low real cost.
- Try to change the timing of the deal, bringing implementation forward and/or improving small payment terms (fast payment in cash, for example, may 'win' an early settlement discount).

Making a large or generous concession is not always the best solution to winning a difficult argument.

Avoid at all costs the thought that a concession made now will be remembered by the other party in your next deal. In such cases, people usually have short memories. In any case, the parties involved may not even be in the same roles when the time comes for future negotiations.

A stalemate position (for example over a complaint or dispute) could lead to legal action. This could bring further consequences – example:

- fast-growing legal fees
- uncertainty over whether the case will influence current and future business activity
- risk of negative publicity
- loss of business confidence in the organization
- possibility of public humiliation.

How personality can influence the status quo

An important element of persuasion and influence is personality, a factor that is easily overlooked when considering the strength or weakness of a case. It can also help to explain how some people seem able to achieve acceptable results from unpromising situations.

So how is *your* charisma? Do you have a warm, mostly happy, outlook on life and, in general discussions, are you positive, optimistic and charming? People who are naturally inclined to be this way start out with something of an advantage, especially if they are able to rise above the irritating factors that drag many people down.

It is sometimes argued that such elements are a matter of birth and heritage – and reinforced by our early upbringing. A warm extrovert will generally achieve much better overall results with other people than those who are pessimistic and depressive.

Can we change?

Yes, simply by becoming more people-centred and exercising more self-control. What is, perhaps, less fair is that above-average performers may also have been endowed with the gift of charisma; this special quality in their personality seems to lead everyone to want to agree with them and they are, generally, highly valued by their organizations.

Of all the basic personality factors that are essential to negotiators the following are the most relevant:

Authority and persistence

We all recognize that authority inside an organization has to be under some control: the Sales Representative is responsible to the Sales Manager and then to the appropriate functional Director; the Board of Directors is responsible to the Chairman, who is answerable to the shareholders.

A consequence of this structure is that we also know that our level in the hierarchy determines our freedom to exercise authority, to make commitments to delivery dates, to agree advantageous prices and so on. Without such controls, there could never be a coherent strategy inside the business. However, we also appreciate that, if there was no element of discretion present, senior managers and directors would never be able to manage, as they would be engaged in the very negotiations that are delegated to their professional staff.

TIP *High achievers in negotiation tend to be people who do not easily accept 'no' for an answer. They persist in seeking to change a 'no' into 'not just now', with the expectation that situations change and an agreement will come in time.*

Task-centred or people-centred influence

Negotiators need to have sufficient technical knowledge of the case in hand or to be accompanied by an expert to enable discussion and the weight of argument to be understood and valued appropriately.

It is sometimes a matter of intense frustration among task negotiators that people-centred influence breaks down barriers and leads the way to agreement. In some of the most intractable disputes, the protagonists become so entrenched that the only way to reach agreement is by replacing the negotiators themselves.

In the search for a balanced team, another strategy would be for the negotiation to be undertaken by two participants: a technical person along with someone more people-centred. There may be additional costs involved in this, as well as the need for trust and 'technique experience' to be built up between the team members so that they do not find themselves in disagreement in front of their opponents.

TIP *Advance notice should always be given to opponents that there will be a team of negotiators rather than an individual, so that they do not feel that this is a rather pressurizing tactic.*

Open-minded or close-minded

One of the consequences of preparing a negotiating strategy is that the key players can become entrenched in their positions. If you suffer from this tendency, ask yourself how you could become more open-minded and what stands in the way. Is it one or more of the following factors?

- politics
- money
- attitudes
- prejudices
- emotions
- money
- greed

The costs incurred could be totally out of proportion to the cost of resolving the problem and, even if blame might be shared, could a solution simply be an unconditional apology or concession?

Tactics

Some negotiators like to prepare a game plan, complete with a set of tactics whose aim is to manipulate their opponents into acceptance. Highly skilled negotiators avoid such approaches since manipulation implies a win/lose strategy that could easily rebound.

There are some basics that, if ignored, can easily generate a negative (or even destructive) atmosphere for meetings. It might be thought that there are some psychological advantages to 'home games', but these can work against you if things go wrong – for example, if distractions or interruptions put the home team at a disadvantage and give additional confidence to the visitors.

Similar results can occur if one team tries to plan a strategy based on a scripted response. (For example, 'When they say "price increase" we will not respond, but will merely nod and immediately walk out for a recess.') This is a plan that could easily go wrong.

 TIP *Straightforward, natural, businesslike behaviour is best – and much less likely to generate problems.*

Stalemate

Stalemate can often happen in a negotiation: the two sides fail to reach agreement, they retire (free to fight again) but the lack of a deal indicates a lose/lose outcome. A supplier fails to win the contract while the client fails to achieve the improved service or facility that had been sought. Of course, failure to agree could have serious results in another few months when the whole contract is up for renewal and the reluctant party discovers that the other side is now looking to change partners.

Such an outcome can be common for salespeople who, by the very nature of their roles, need to be optimistic. As a consequence, they may fail to qualify prospects thoroughly, leading to time and energy invested in a negotiation that later falls apart.

Team-building

Negotiating in teams (even of two people) requires full commitment to achieving a win/win result – before, during, and after the meeting. Any hint of weakness (even a non-verbal signal from one individual in a team meeting) may invite a negative reaction from the opposing team.

The leader must create team motivation by:

- briefing team members thoroughly, so that they are fully committed to the 'party line'
- taking care to listen to any objections or worries and addressing these sensitively
- casting the team so that even junior members have a positive role.

SUNDAY

MONDAY

TUESDAY

WEDNESDAY

THURSDAY

FRIDAY

SATURDAY

TIP

Behaviour in public should ideally be neutral. In session, however, it should be outwardly positive and always showing support of team leaders and their stance.

Negotiating in teams: casting

How large should a team be? The ideal size depends upon the nature of the project and the extent to which specialists might be needed in the team.

Roles that may be needed in a sizeable team include:

● **Leader**, responsible for:
  - opening the meeting
  - setting and promoting the agenda
  - managing and co-ordinating the team (directing who speaks and when)
  - orchestrating specialist input as necessary
  - summarizing (as and when necessary) and closing the meeting
● **Deputy leader**, responsible for:
  - supporting the leader, with notes and prompts if and when needed
  - monitoring the time, especially to help trigger recesses
  - standing in for the leader if necessary
● **Secretary/note-taker**, responsible for:
  - taking notes of the key points made by both parties (particularly important later when it comes to checking who said what and when)
  - ensuring that proposals and agreements accepted are not diluted or lost in later discussion
● **Specialist(s)**, responsible for:
  - supporting the team's case with technical inputs as and when required by the leader
● **Observer(s)**, responsible for:
  - studying selected members of the opposing team, in order to note facial expressions, body language and so on, for discussion in the team during formal recesses.

These team roles may be concentrated into fewer hands, especially if facilities and time resources are in short supply. The size of the team in more dramatic scenarios, such as a labour dispute or a legal dispute between a board of directors and a plaintiff team, could be rather larger.

A vital feature of team negotiations is that team members follow a prescribed code of behaviour:

- The team leader must be respected at all times.
- Team members must speak only when directed or invited to do so and with the leader's agreement.
- Each member must stick strictly to the team's agreed strategy.

Time – the limited resource

Remember that the more people there are involved in meetings the less likely it is that time will be used wisely. If each of the five roles mentioned above are mirrored in the other team and each person spends, say, three minutes asking a question and three minutes receiving a detailed reply, this would take over an hour and would probably see very little progress made.

Furthermore, if emotions are running high, the necessary disciplines of one person speaking at a time and everyone else listening can easily disappear, leading to 'multi-speak chaos' and nobody listening!

Should this occur the best response is to call a recess.

The recess

Calling a recess can be valuable for:

- consulting the team about current progress or suitability of offers
- checking progress against the team's agenda
- gaining feedback from observations of the opposing team
- checking on so-called facts quoted by the opposition
- restoring order in the team.

The timing of recesses can be critical – if they come too soon and are too frequent, it can make the leader look lacking in self-confidence; if they are infrequent (or non-existent), it can leave other team members feeling overlooked and undervalued.

Summary

Proposals and concessions lie at the heart of negotiations and the best results come from being able to balance objectives and concessions on both sides. Such exchanges can be interpreted as both 'wins' and 'concessions', depending upon the starting points, but the most important outcome is that the final agreement is accepted as a close match to the objectives prepared by either side. This can be described as a win/win result. Keeping a clear head is vital as any explicit excitement could lead to serious mistakes and exceptions, which may lead to further negotiation later.

Now you have completed Wednesday's study, complete the 'progress check' and then turn to the end of the book and make a commitment to your Personal Action Plan.

SUNDAY
MONDAY
TUESDAY
WEDNESDAY
THURSDAY
FRIDAY
SATURDAY

Progress check (answers at the back)

1. A process proposal is one that:
   a) Sets a value on the subject currently under discussion ❏
   b) The leading party can choose to make to start the meeting ❏
   c) Will be instantly adopted by both parties ❏
   d) Either party can make about the processes in the meeting ❏

2. In a complex negotiating situation that results in a stalemate, the most important quality for the negotiator to apply is:
   a) Persistence ❏
   b) A sense of humour ❏
   c) His/her power to impose an agreement ❏
   d) Patience ❏

3. A concession is:
   a) Something already built into a proposal at the quoted price or value ❏
   b) A special change to the proposal that represents a reduction in the quoted price ❏
   c) An allowance that has the appearance of increasing the cost of an item ❏
   d) A reduction imposed on both sides by an external authority ❏

4. A prepared game-plan runs the risk of chaos if it goes wrong. It is far better to aim to:
   a) Build up trust between the parties through a sense of humour ❏
   b) Reduce the tension by providing a regular supply of refreshments ❏
   c) Be better at gamesmanship ❏
   d) Project the image of being a trusted and experienced businessperson ❏

5. A counter-proposal is:
   a) A statement that differs from an opponent's proposal and follows on immediately from it ❏
   b) Any proposal that is stated in an apologetic way, seeking to avoid a major disagreement with your opponent ❏
   c) A contradictory statement that will lead into a defence/attack spiral ❏
   d) A way to express the inner feelings of either negotiator ❏

6. An above-average negotiator is someone who:
   a) Has persistence and a sense of humour ❏
   b) Is completely task-centred ❏
   c) Is authoritative, people-centred and open-minded ❏
   d) Has a grasp of winning tactics ❏

7. The number of participants in a negotiating team is best limited to:
a) A maximum of two on each side ❏
b) The leader and any specialists who may need to be present ❏
c) The leader plus four others ❏
d) Any number providing all present stick closely to a pre-agreed strategy ❏

8. It is important to avoid a stalemate position in a negotiation because:
a) It will reflect badly on the two negotiators involved ❏
b) Each negotiator will be accused of being inflexible ❏
c) Changing the negotiators would be the alternative ❏
d) A subsequent negative outcome could result in a serious loss of face ❏

9. The best way of enhancing negotiating skills is through:
a) Understanding the theories and practising them in a learning simulation ❏
b) Learning on the job ❏
c) Testing out the theories by talking to experienced negotiators ❏
d) Being committed to continuous improvement ❏

10. 'Let's aim to agree and sign the contract by 5 p.m.' is:
a) An enhanced concept ❏
b) A disagreement ❏
c) An improvement point ❏
d) A process proposal ❏

THURSDAY

Problem-solving through consulting and listening skills

General guidelines can easily overlook challenges posed by real human beings. To dismiss such difficulties as just the normal challenges created by people can mean failing to seek practical solutions. Individuals are usually at the heart of disputes and, if filled with the deep conviction that they are right, they can provide a real and powerful obstacle to organizational change and improvement.

Today's theme is all about creating change through discussion and debate, which can be crucial when a negotiation is taking place to achieve measurable and lasting change.

We will cover techniques that are highly desirable – as well as those that, if used, may poison the atmosphere for years to come! The aim should always be to achieve a collaborative atmosphere, discarding those techniques that may deliver quick wins but also leave opponents seeking to fight back on another day.

It is very important that obstacles are not allowed to become hostages to fortune; careless or unpleasant treatment of individuals can generate ill-feeling and a lack of trust that can take a generation to overcome. This is especially true when a workforce has trade union representation, although this does at least provide a route for problems to be represented and debated. Where no such official route exists, complaints can create general resentment, demotivation and even an increase in labour turnover. This, however, is an argument for better, and timely, listening, not for giving in to every demand or request.

Often, the instigator of a dispute starts by being loud, demanding and even offensive because they believe that it is the only way to have their case heard. An uninterrupted hearing, accompanied by patience and a lack of defensiveness, will remove some of the sharp emotion; calm discussion can then lead to a realistic response to the problem.

A greater difficulty arises when human need confronts the organization's system. In such cases, making an exception can work only as a very last resort, because it is possible that everyone else in the organization will demand equal rights. Such difficulties will test the patience of most managers, especially those who have a strong commitment to maintaining output, production, sales and so on. So mediation may be needed in the search for creative solutions to intransigent problems.

Resolving problems through consulting and listening

While it might not be your official role to intercede or counsel colleagues, such opportunities obviously offer the chance to practise interpersonal skills that are also useful in negotiation sessions, especially when the negotiation turns out to revolve around problems relating to systems, failed service or interpersonal relations.

On Sunday we described ten priority roles and invited readers to use the self-rating scale. We shall now revisit the same tool with a view to identifying colleagues' or friends'

profiles. It is always possible to try to emulate their preferred style, though you might find that this only reinforces their prejudices or attitudes, which may not be helpful in your negotiations in the future.

Go back now to the the series of tasks set in Sunday's chapter but this time nominate the individual whose attitudes are typified by each particular topic. Write in their name and then, on the scale, circle your interpretation of their score. This exercise could equally apply to any other individuals whom you know well, perhaps within your family or circle of friends.

The purpose of this exercise is to increase sensitivity to each characteristic and consider how we might be able to influence opinions and ideas through the use of one of the other styles. The aim is to change attitudes and encourage the adoption of a more constructive view.

Seeking movement

Wherever and whenever we negotiate, the chances that we will collide with the attitudes and ideas of others are high – that is, after all, the basis of the need to negotiate in the first place. At its simplest level, it may be that tabled proposals are not acceptable to the other party (although sometimes the rejection is as much to do with the person who is promoting the idea). So, let us now consider some of the barriers to agreement, and explore alternative tactics that may produce constructive movement and ultimate agreement.

Removing listening barriers

Ask yourself the following questions:

- Am I communicating in commonly understood language?
- Could it have been 'corrupted' by double meanings or prejudice?
- Is the way I speak (for example, my choice of words and/or my voice) appealing, or is it provocative?

- Did I correctly identify the best selling points (features and benefits)?
- Was my communication punchy and persuasive, or was it wordy and confusing?
- Did I eradicate irritators (words, phrases and gestures)?
- Did my body language aid listeners' concentration, or did it distract them?
- Were there distractions such as external events and noise?
- Did I make change seem natural rather than competitive, irrational or threatening?
- Did we attract (influential) individuals on to our side?
- Did we spell out the (costly/dangerous/unacceptable) results of not adopting the proposed changes?

TIP *In real-life bargaining sessions, could you be unwittingly creating or reinforcing prejudices and objections simply by the way we talk to your people?*

Improving the atmosphere in bargaining sessions

The overall climate in our organization may be hindering change, and consideration may need to be given to some steps that could help to change that. The following is a checklist of questions to ask yourself that may uncover additional points for change:

- Are we meeting proposals sharply with counter-proposals rather than presenting them as new ideas?
- Are we labelling our disagreement (e.g. regularly stating 'I disagree with you there'), which serves only to underline conflict in our positions?
- Can we remove physical and human barriers (e.g. table blocks, ranking, perks that underline hierarchy and so on)?
- Have we fallen into the trap of defence/attack spirals (where one statement is immediately followed by a riposte

that puts forward the opposite, for example pay increase – pay cut)?

- Do we regularly use 'why' questions, which can suggest aggression? The softer question construction would be 'How did you come to that decision?', and not 'Why do you think that?'
- How are we able to demonstrate differences between fact and opinion? Facts may be unpleasant but they can be handled and managed without conflict; opinions vary and can be formed from opposite forces, providing raw fuel for conflict.
- Do we invite an attack on our proposals by diluting our own case through listing a number of weak arguments in the mistaken belief that more is best? This incurs the risk of our opponent climbing up the list, successfully attacking each one in turn, with the possible outcome being that the top (and best) argument is eclipsed and even destroyed once all the others have been easily rebutted.

TIP *Skilled negotiators regularly review their methods to focus on those that are most appropriate to the needs, people and outcomes achieved.*

Creative solutions for problem situations

Managers have to manage change, and the success of this is likely to depend on the willingness and enthusiasm of those who have to implement it. For this reason, it is worth investing time in preparing and strengthening your case. Consider the following questions:

- Will the change help us through short-, medium- or long-term situations? If so, how?
- How can we separate the various interests involved in the change – for example clients, suppliers, operators, services and so on – and emphasize the benefits to each of them?

Behaviours to exploit

Here is a reminder of the key negotiating behaviours and techniques used by top negotiators:

Trial proposals

An example is: 'Suppose we were able to build into the agreement a condition that all management and staff will be guaranteed job security for six months after the takeover? Would that help to allay everyone's fears?' A positive response could then lead to a more formal or definite version which could be recorded in an 'If... then...' format.

Timing

Once again, timing can be critical to success – offering too little, too late is one criticism often applied in industrial disputes. The worry is that any offer may be used as an excuse for the opposing team to increase their own demands even further, as the interpretation may be that 'as management feels obliged to make an offer, we can exploit their weak position by seeking even more benefits'. This is not a helpful response, of course, and could result in the earlier proposition being hastily withdrawn – especially if it threatens the very scheme, transaction or reputation that the organization has been developing.

Motivators of conflict

There is often a feeling that a good argument would be entertaining – a break from the everyday routine. What is not always understood is that, once out of the box, conflict can be both destructive and difficult to resolve and can lead to a game of brinkmanship. Let us examine the motivators of conflict more closely:

Levers

A lever can be used by either side in a dispute to obtain resolution of a long-standing problem (even if it is actually unrelated). To motivate an agreement on the larger stage, in a more important deal, a long-sought demand is conceded. Clearly, lack of progress on either front might not lead to a stoppage but could certainly be classed as a lose/lose position.

Defeat or humiliation

Sometimes a dispute arises simply because the issue involved has become the last straw. Perhaps concessions have already been made by both sides – almost as a gesture of goodwill – but now the aggrieved party feels obliged to fight simply because they feel boxed in, with little alternative but to give in yet again. This could be the ultimate humiliation.

Retaliation

This may seem the most childish motivator of all and is based on the tit-for-tat behaviour we all probably witnessed in our early years. Some adults still think in this way and, although they may not reach an all-out dispute, the consequences can be extremely irritating, such as a voluntary ban on overtime working or the strict application of safety procedures that have become more flexible in everyday operation.

Thin end of the wedge

This strategy may bring stronger resistance if one side feels that relatively minor demands or changes – if accepted – may result in much greater demands next time. This may sound typical of industrial relations but can just as easily apply to terms and conditions of a contract (such as minimum order quantities, pack sizes and so on).

Deterrent

The very risk of one party withdrawing support from another – and the consequential loss of a high-profile image or technical reputation – may cause the main contractor to take a flexible approach on such issues as visiting staff using the car park, the use of the director's box at the football club and so on. No one wants to upset this much-prized client or joint-project company. Such pressure points may be unspoken – but they are very real.

Guerrilla warfare

Again, this potentially destructive strategy is probably more suspected of taking place in today's world rather than actually doing so. However, it might occur when one party, such as a staff association or trade union, has such a strong hatred of the current system that they will sponsor almost any breach of the organization's system. The aim can be expressed as 'Everyone knows it's already broken – so let's get it fixed once and for all.' The management team will be very reluctant to change the system because they know that it will trigger a significant increase in costs. The situation could feel like a guerrilla war – enacted sporadically.

> **TIP** *You may well recognize some, if not all, of the above examples, which can become major distractions from meaningful work and productivity. The main aim should be to avoid lose/lose outcomes by addressing the fundamental issues and negotiating them out.*

Conflict – the result of competing objectives

From the viewpoint of positive influence, conflict is clearly a dilution of energy that would be better dedicated to the achievement of the ultimate objectives of the organization. However, problems do occur from time to time and there is a risk that, without professional support, matters can get worse and even end up in legal sanctions. Conflicts, without support or intervention, can follow a progressive sequence and cause very unfortunate results: initially anxiety, progressing to loss of self-esteem, then depression, a persecution complex, the loss of any sense of reality, and finally withdrawal and burnout.

Psychological games

We have seen above how groups can, effectively, hold an organization hostage. This section covers a similar theme but is concerned with the one-on-one relationship between two individuals, for example a sales representative and a buyer. In each case, there is a potential misuse of power or discomfort, led by the person who thinks that the behaviour provides a motivator for the opponent to make additional concessions.

- **High seat/low seat:** readers may recall this method being used in the school headmaster's study: 'I am in control here in my high seat. You have little or none, so you are in a low seat.' A rather obvious act of resistance to this tactic is to plead a bad back and reverse the tactic by standing up!
- **Irritators:** a well-respected retail buyer, renowned for his professionalism, impeccable hygiene and appearance, reviewed a new product range to be stocked in the supplier's prestigious showroom while sniffing loudly all the way round, a behaviour which would be recognized as impolite. Why did he do this? Maybe the irritator motivated the sales manager to help him make some rapid choices, with a generous trade discount, and then make a hasty exit?
- **Defence/attack:** these pair of behaviours can quickly descend into playground politics, with the same risk that the name-calling could get out of hand! What might start out as a fun distraction could end up in a defence/attack spiral that has all the intensity of an arm-wrestling match.
- **Blocking:** habitual blockers are very difficult to deal with; they engage in very little interaction and block discussion with just a few words: 'Can't do that!'; 'There's no point!' Discussion is thus at a dead end. The situation is all the more annoying if this is the only person you can deal with. The solution is to find a new contact and an irrefutable reason for a discussion.

- **Argument dilution:** the user of this behaviour openly lists all the reasons (both good and bad) to support a proposal, which allows the opponent to destroy all the weak arguments and begin to weaken even the stronger ones. This is not a recommended strategy for either player.
- **Unrealistic timescales:** *Buyer:* 'I'd agree to this proposal if you could get the delivery here tomorrow!' *Seller:* 'I can't promise that – our deliveries aren't due to arrive until next month!' *Buyer:* 'Well, that's out then!'
- **Shut-outs:** a shut-out is similar to 'blocking'; the strategy is designed to close down discussion and probably bring the meeting to an end. It is very difficult to react positively to this behaviour except by approaching someone else in the organization. The speaker is almost saying 'See my boss'. If you do, you may not make any better progress, but it is worth trying.

Continuous improvement

A major gain from practical negotiation training programmes is that debate and argument can be tested in a simulation. The strength of a case can be tested through a role-playing exercise, and with professional facilitation and support, as well as with the addition of video-recording, tactical debating skills can be polished.

A key advantage of this form of development is that teamwork can be orchestrated constructively and the ways in which proposals are made can be reviewed for their credibility and potential for improvement. The final learning power lies in being able to obtain honest feedback from opposing teams – and to be able to compare results against the plans made.

This is not rocket science: most top negotiators have benefited from this kind of experience before taking on top management assignments that involve takeovers, mergers and acquisitions as well as major contracting, purchasing or marketing projects.

Summary

Today we have reviewed one of the most difficult aspects of negotiation, which luckily occurs only infrequently. The main aim of all high-profile negotiators is a trouble-free negotiation that leads to profitable repeat business on that contract on a continuous basis. Those who find themselves having to keep renegotiating existing agreements may well be doing something wrong.

Normally, negotiators should be encouraged to follow these sequential steps:

1 observation
2 analysis and diagnosis
3 test negotiation
4 analysis of problem/opportunity
5 application
6 results
7 review.

Following these should ensure that negotiators learn from their negotiating experience – and avoid repeating any behavioural mistakes.

Now you have completed Thursday's chapter, complete the 'progress check' on the next page and then turn to the end of the book and make a commitment to your Personal Action Plan.

SUNDAY
MONDAY
TUESDAY
WEDNESDAY
THURSDAY
FRIDAY
SATURDAY

Progress check (answers at the back)

1. Problems in organizations are a natural consequence of bringing together a rich mix of people. Managers need to:
   a) Confront the causes of problems and any mischievous or disruptive people ❏
   b) Consult any representative body for accurate information ❏
   c) Provide a briefing session for line managers ❏
   d) Listen for feedback from trusted spokespersons ❏

2. Individuals' preferred roles lead to ways in which listening and consulting could:
   a) Help persuade them to be more adaptable to new situations ❏
   b) Provide challenges to their usual way of thinking ❏
   c) Help them analyse and promote new ways of handling problems ❏
   d) Resolve difficulties and regain control ❏

3. Interpersonal skills that are valuable in negotiation situations are:
   a) Listening to the case that is presented ❏
   b) Analysing the case ❏
   c) Absorbing the emotions that have been used ❏
   d) All of the above ❏

4. An extrovert will respond best to a:
   a) Good listener ❏
   b) Controller ❏
   c) Politician ❏
   d) Completer/Finisher ❏

5. The mix that is most likely to result in a noisy disagreement is:
   a) Expert/Teacher and Pessimist ❏
   b) Safety first and Completer/Finisher ❏
   c) Opportunist and Controller ❏
   d) Naive and Politician ❏

6. An example of a listening barrier is a:
   a) Foreign language ❏
   b) Corrupted meaning ❏
   c) Defence/attack expression ❏
   d) Counter-proposal ❏

7. Obtaining a constructive hearing is enabled by:
   a) Making change seem natural and easy ❏
   b) Not being prepared to discuss the objections ❏
   c) Holding the discussion when there are many distractions ❏
   d) Using known irritators ❏

8. Psychological games in negotiation:

a) Provide valuable additional pressure to achieve acceptance of your proposals ❑

b) Include a risk that the games could backfire on the negotiator ❑

c) Are a poor persuasion method that risks total rejection of the case and the opponent ❑

d) Can involve permissible put-downs of the opponent's case ❑

9. Top negotiators work towards:

a) Building up their personal reputation as sharp negotiators ❑

b) Beating opponents by destroying their case ❑

c) Winning every case and building up a personal 100-per-cent track record of implementation ❑

d) Coping with the renegotiation of existing agreements when demanded by opponents ❑

10. Skilled negotiators build up their reputation as trusted operators by

a) Resisting the temptation of building an extreme personal reputation as a 'guru' ❑

b) Concentrating efforts on building a track record of continuing success ❑

c) Avoiding having to reopen cases once they have been agreed and settled ❑

d) Ensuring that they are never caught out as a two-faced negotiator ❑

FRIDAY

What if? – closing skills

Most negotiators experience self-doubt at some time, which can lead to two possible consequences:

1 a slow-down in the pace of the discussion (almost expressing a reluctance to close the agreement in case the deal is deficient in some way)
2 a complete disengagement through a fear of some hidden trap that would lose all benefits from an agreement.

These anxieties are entirely normal, and today we will examine approaches that should help bring closure:

● The power of personality
● How to handle remaining differences
● Using probing skills, for example 'What if...?'
● Managing negative behaviours at the close
● Using creative solutions to bring about a successful close
● Avoiding common tricks.

Now we have moved to the critical end game. Closing the deal should entail arriving at a logical result, a predictable outcome. You may have a sense of anticipation, and perhaps even excitement, but it is best to keep these emotions out of your mind as over-confidence may generate client concern and worry that a legal contract might involve something of a 'catch'. If you find closing off a negotiation difficult or embarrassing, ask yourself:

- What if I am unable to close this deal? What might happen?
- Who else might be involved (for example, a competitor)?
- What if I had allowed more/less time and/or given more/ fewer concessions?

If you are asking yourself these questions now, be aware that these factors should have been discovered much earlier in the relationship by simply asking a question such as 'Who else might be in the frame for this contract? ... We appreciate that our clients have a choice about who they may choose as their suppliers – it would be very interesting to know who else they might be talking to about this project.'

Power of personality

Your personality should be your best tool in helping close the meeting successfully. How you present yourself is an important expression of your personality and can provide a signal of what to expect in conversation. The way in which we greet other people is important: our manners are on show and this is especially important if the meeting involves cross-cultural issues. Cultural sensitivities may be vital, so some specialist advice might be required.

Tact and courtesy are essential, especially in any 'warm-up' conversation. Your opponents – like you – may appear to be entirely relaxed and self-controlled, but changes occur as the deal is finally constructed and agreed. Smiles all round are normal, but pressure might have created nervous tension. This is a good opportunity to relax over a cup of coffee or a drink. Once relaxed, your opponents may tell you what those tensions were about and you can address them.

TIP *Be prepared to handle some potentially tricky issues –*
especially if your organization has an 'awkward' track
record.

Avoiding failure and embarrassment

All closing methods are perfectly workable, but some
professionals still do not use them. Why? Because of a
simple fear of rejection. If you are unsure if the deal is
heading towards a green light, then be prepared to keep
talking, but be careful that you don't talk yourself out of a
deal altogether.

If you are sure that the deal is good, ask the closing
question: 'So, are we ready to close and sign off this
agreement?' One 'yes!' and the deal is done. Be careful,
however, that the question does not sound either too relaxed,
too assertive or, worst of all, wheedling or scared. Your timing
is vital – premature closure could still lose you the deal.

Remaining differences

At this stage, your opponents may still not be explicitly
declaring complete support for this deal – which can be quite
unnerving – and your own conversational style could create
more difficulties. For example, a high reactor may be tempted
into a lengthy dose of cross-check questioning:

Question	Response
How do you feel about all this?	OK! (*Not much of an answer!*)
It must feel good to have it almost over?	I suppose so. (*Still a minimal response!*)
Now is the time to say if you have any concerns!	Well, there's not much to say. (*Still little response!*)

(*Continued*)

Question	Response
So, do you think this is a fair result? I know that *we* are happy.	Of course you are; you've got everything you wanted, I'm sure! Now we see how your business makes so much profit in a recession. I doubt we'll ever be back for another deal like this — or any other, come to that!

Such an attack might seem to be over-aggressive – especially after the minimal involvement of the person during the earlier discussion. If the leader of the meeting is really a very democratic person who strongly believes in the win/win style, the outburst could feel like a sudden shower of icy water. It could also lead to the person inviting the opponent to state their preferred outcome (which could then bring about a very different result).

Question	Response
Is this really likely to happen?	Yes, it could!
Would a win/win outcome be better?	Definitely!

The question that the example raises is whether the approach illustrated is genuine or whether the speaker saw the opportunity to lead the discussion into a win/lose situation, with the tactical aim of coming out on top right at the finishing line.

Probing skills: Who? What? How? When? Where? Why?

Top negotiators find the use of probing skills very valuable. This umbrella term describes the use of a series of open questions. The six question words themselves are non-threatening and generally bring detailed responses from low reactors, which is very helpful in describing needs and wants.

TIP *The 'why?' question is rather more assertive (and can even border on the aggressive), and may need to be rephrased if a collaborative atmosphere is valued.*

If there are still some outstanding issues, the following summary should help:

1 Isolate the issues by asking the other party to summarize them – and listen carefully!
2 Check this list against your own understanding of the objectives, any notes taken, and any concessions agreed from earlier conversations.
3 Work through the items, checking first that there is no misunderstanding that needs addressing.
4 Once this is done, the scale of any difference between the two sides will be clear and a final gesture may be all that is needed to close (it would be best if this can still be phrased as a conditional offer, i.e. 'If... then...').

TIP

If a minor concession at the close of the deal maintains a valuable long-term relationship, then it will have been a worthwhile gesture.

Negative behaviours at the close

Top negotiators try to avoid negative thinking and behaviour (both in preparation and in final meetings). This does not mean that they seek to make forward progress regardless of the weight of opinion, preferring to offer a plan B and try to keep options open. When a goal – and a route – have been chosen, positive energy should arise and fast progress will make plans a reality. Any doubts expressed by the manager, colleagues and even team members may be heard but now rejected as 'negative thinking'. When approaching closing sequences, negotiators need to be alert to any hint of negative signals, which may reinforce the need for caution.

Here is a reminder of those influences:

● **Argument dilution:** the tendency to give multiple reasons for an action when only the best may be needed to make the point. Mixing weak arguments encourages opponents to attack the weakest ones and, by inference, arranging all the negative points suggests that it might be better to wait until a better option comes along ('Maybe my critics were right' is the winning thought). In short, the energy has gone out of the positive argument and the deal may be lost.

- **Defence/attack:** extraordinary though it might seem, there are some negotiators who, even at the threshold of a new agreement, cannot resist the opportunity to attack a past behaviour of the other side. This might be related to a complaint, a failed initiative, or having been let down by a team member. Such approaches run the risk of diluting enthusiasm for the current deal and can be seen as a form of 'one-upmanship'.

- **Blocking:** close to agreement an opponent may still seem to block further progress in the debate. This may be a conversational habit that they are unaware of. Either way, comments such as 'It won't work', 'It's not worth it', or 'We'll probably be back round the table in a few months still trying to fix it' may be partly said in jest but, again, can dilute vital energy for the intended deal and are therefore best avoided.

- **Shutting out:** this is impolite behaviour involving one person talking over another before they have completed a sentence or idea. This might be because they find their delivery slow, predictable or weak. Try to be more disciplined and let the other party finish before speaking. If you fear that a long-winded partner will cause you to forget the point you wanted to make, write a brief note so that you can pick up your thread when the moment comes. (Being lectured at for 30 minutes is a sure-fire way of creating a determination not to close the deal today.)

- **Irritators:** at a lower scale, irritators can also create negative reactions and, in combination with any of the items above, can contribute to failure.

- **Exaggeration:** it is probably inevitable that those who are most in favour of a deal feel the need to impress their opponent with their experience, importance (to their own organization), past deals set up and negotiated, high-profile people they have met, and glamorous places they have been. Such behaviour is likely to be viewed as boastful and, again, can be very wearing. On its own, however, it might not be a reason for ditching a deal, unless some of the boasting is known to be totally untrue.

TIP *Try to cope with these obstacles: have a close friend help you make a list of any irritants you use in conversation and then try to get them under control.*

Creative solutions to difficult problems

Whatever the tension, try to relax and focus on the professional need to close this deal with all the *i*s dotted and *t*s crossed, and remember that not all negotiations are fresh, positive and potentially profitable. Some have to deal with less pleasant topics, such as complaints, failures or upsets, and so there may be a very stark choice: reach some kind of agreement that is acceptable to both sides or go to law!

Resolving disputes using a third party can be far better – and considerably less expensive – provided that both sides are prepared to invest effort in reaching a compromise. An unhealthy determination to win and 'punish' the other side might prove counterproductive.

Top negotiators can find themselves in weak positions when a negative news story concerning their company breaks right in the middle of a vital negotiation. After the fuss has died down, the fact is that both sides still have needs that must be satisfied and one can argue that no organization is likely to be right in all that it does 100 per cent of the time.

Closing – the natural resolution

We have explored the effect of irritators and how they can wind opponents up, sometimes unconsciously. When it comes to closing, there is a possibility that an opponent might deliberately create pressure to soften up the opponent with the objective of prising more concessions from them. There is obviously the danger that such behaviour could lead the negotiator into the decision to break off all relations – that is, the result is lose/lose.

Many negotiators concentrate on just one or two easily identifiable closing approaches. Although many sales and marketing professionals are taught eight different ways in which to close a deal, most focus on just the one or two ways that they are most comfortable with.

Meetings can stall because of the following:

- things becoming too long-winded
- resistance created from a mistimed attempt to close, which leads to more objections or queries indicating that the other party is feeling less confident that this deal is right for them
- a time-out has occurred and one party has to leave the meeting.

However, good conversationalists can quickly disperse discomfort or embarrassment and, more often than not, still reach a positive result. Top negotiators are able to gain an insight into how close they might be to the finishing line by asking the question: 'How are you feeling about the progress we have made so far?'

The best approaches

The predecessor to this book, *Negotiation Skills In A Week*, provided detailed advice on five methods of closing a deal:

1 Close any gaps.
2 Time and timing: this needs sensitivity. Too long is boring; too short can feel pushy and may be thought to be offensive.
3 Either/or choice: a softer option ('no deal' is not on offer).
4 Last concession: a riskier approach – who says it is the last concession?
5 Recess: time to think it over may be helpful. If you offer this, stay close by so that you can handle other queries and watch that your opponent doesn't gradually lose momentum and interest.

In this book, I focus instead on simplicity in closing. However, there remains one vital element that must apply in all circumstances: both sides must fully understand and be committed to the detailed deal before parting. This is where trouble can arise: there may be a demand or promise made that actually lies outside the negotiator's authority to trade. The professional way of handling this would be to call a recess, check it out and then conclude.

> **TIP** It is vital that these additional processes do not siphon off all the good energy and enthusiasm that has brought the parties to the point of agreement.

But what if the vital authority is unavailable to confirm and authorize the issue? You might have to agree here and now on the condition that approval is confirmed in writing after the meeting. In other words, a Memorandum of Understanding must be prepared and acknowledged rather than a full contractual agreement. The disadvantage of this kind of process is that, once the negotiators have parted, the door is open for another round of potential negotiation to be undertaken by the specialists, who may have to handle non-implementation matters in the case of a dispute.

Take care with some common tricks

Closing is the ultimate indicator of commitment and it provides a real test of everyone's integrity. Unfortunately, there are those who may see this step as an opportunity to use fast-talking tactics, leading to confusion and acceptance where rejection would have been a more conservative decision. Here are five of the more common sharp tactics that should be avoided:

1 **The mis-summary:** here, the 'pushy' party deliberately gives a verbal summary that is accepted and turns out to have better terms than given in the formal written contract that the other party will sign. Always check the paperwork thoroughly and reject it if it does not say what you have agreed.
2 **Bullying/blocking/shutting out:** these are not good behaviours but are sometimes used by desperate people.

No matter how attractive the offer is, if you are uncomfortable with these tactics, refuse the deal. This is where having an alternative potential supplier, customer and so on gives you hidden power.

3 **Promoting false deadlines:** as a means of pushing the deal through, the opponent might link bad news about an extended delivery or implementation time to a promotional price (this might be 'special' but how could you check it?).

4 **Misuse of recesses:** what is the purpose of a recess? We would expect that the recess gives both parties the opportunity to make a final check: 'Shall we go ahead, or can anyone think of a reason why going ahead might lead to trouble?' Additional pressure can be put on a nervous opponent by seeming to be a reluctant client or supplier, and calling an additional recess may be an indicator of more uncertainty or reluctance. The response of some anxious opponents might be to make yet another concession in order to clinch the deal.

5 **Building trust with success stories with other businesses or industries:** sharing successful project experiences as a means of promoting the next deal is a common approach used by negotiators. However, such self-promotion should probably be listened to politely but with some scepticism.

Who is the best survivor now?

After all this effort, which negotiator profile is most likely to be successful at the close of the negotiation? On Sunday you read descriptions of ten types of role. Before completing today's study, re-examine the ten profiles in that chapter and answer the following question: Who is likely to be the best at applying the advice given in this book?

Tomorrow we will revisit this with a view to setting out some further developments from the overall process. Before you complete the week's study, think about which of the ten profiles are most likely to achieve a win/win outcome and which are more likely to end a negotiation in stalemate.

Summary

It is often said that the devil is in the detail, which may mean that a negotiated settlement is useful only if it can actually be implemented. We have seen how important it is that both parties are committed to a clear action plan for implementing the agreement, which may be summarized as 'Who is going to do what, to whom? And at what cost?'

Any misunderstandings at this stage may cause entire issues to have to be reopened at yet another negotiation, or – in the worst-case scenario – a complete breakdown in relations, which in turn can lead to the involvement of intermediaries or conciliators, and perhaps even the additional expense of lawyers.

The underlying aim of this book is to create unanimity and business growth through strong partnering and the enhancement of trust through mutually supportive behaviours. Any action or thinking that endangers continuity towards that end should be carefully avoided.

Now complete the 'progress check' on the next page and then turn to the end of the book and make a commitment to your Personal Action Plan.

SUNDAY
MONDAY
TUESDAY
WEDNESDAY
THURSDAY
FRIDAY
SATURDAY

Progress check (answers at the back)

1. Closing techniques provide:
   a) A way of checking to see whether the other party is really interested in the deal in hand ❏
   b) A way of helping to narrow down the options on offer ❏
   c) A fast track to finalizing the deal ❏
   d) The opportunity to obtain feedback from the other party ❏

2. How we present ourselves is an important element in:
   a) Impressing the other party ❏
   b) Personal projection ❏
   c) Impressing the boss ❏
   d) Creating an influential presence for all at the meeting ❏

3. The best emotion to experience as the closing phase of a negotiation is reached is:
   a) Excitement ❏
   b) Caution ❏
   c) Regret ❏
   d) Embarrassment ❏

4. Talking your way through the closing phase of the negotiation could vary because of:
   a) Your opponent's reactor profile ❏
   b) The level of comfort there has been during the meeting ❏
   c) How relaxed and thoughtful your partner feels ❏
   d) Your opponent's reaction on closure ❏

5. Taking into account any cultural sensitivities in your meeting means:
   a) Using non-discriminatory language in the meeting ❏
   b) Offering any refreshments as normal ❏
   c) Using greetings and farewells to all those present as normal ❏
   d) Expecting formal dress from all for a formal meeting ❏

6. Closure means that:
   a) You and your opponents have agreed on 90 per cent of the negotiated deal so that it can be implemented ❏
   b) All parties intend to sign up to the deal as an outcome to the meeting ❏
   c) Thinking space should be claimed before further progress ❏
   d) There would be value in having a final recess before signing up to the deal ❏

7. In a negotiation about payment terms for a supply of services, the consideration of choice of currency for use in payment could be recognized as an outstanding issue and should be:

a) Summarized as an item to be discussed in a special meeting agenda ❏

b) Checked carefully against your original tender document and any misunderstanding clarified ❏

c) Re-summarized by your opponent and compared with your original proposal ❏

d) Identified as a stumbling block that is best overcome by making a concession ❏

8. As the time for closure approaches, stumbling blocks may create a rise in the 'temperature' of the meeting. This could cause intemperate behaviour such as:

a) Making more proposals ❏
b) Summarizing ❏
c) Shutting out the speech of the opposition ❏
d) Reiterating objections to the meeting ❏

9. The vital element that brings a greater chance of reaching that final agreement from the meeting is.

a) Clarifying the gaps ❏
b) Inching towards each other by making minor concessions ❏
c) Trying out new ways to achieve agreement ❏
d) Threatening to pull out if agreement cannot be reached within an imposed deadline ❏

10. A final concession may be:

a) A costly way of luring opponents to agreement ❏
b) An irritation, as the term was not available earlier ❏
c) A new baseline from which the next round of negotiating will start ❏
d) A helpful initiative – but only if emphasized as being available only on this deal and only today! ❏

SATURDAY

Celebrating the successful outcome

Advanced Negotiation Skills In A Week is fast coming to an end but, as a process for you, the reader, it is all about to start!

Together, we have analysed how to improve our results in a field that never fails to intrigue regular negotiators. This is mainly because it is negotiators who link businesses together and contribute in a major way to bottom-line results. This process came to a pinnacle in the last chapter as we closed the deal, so what is left?

This chapter carries an important message for everyone who enjoys the thrill of deal-making – namely, setting up the most difficult challenge of all: celebrating the new agreement and then ensuring that its implementation is carried through in a thoughtful, professional manner.

You will be focusing on:

- the pitfalls that can open up in concluding and implementing the deal
- constraints that can hinder that implementation
- how to support the relationship with supportive monitoring
- maintaining high aspirations while developing partnering skills
- focusing on those behavioural skills that help to create and maintain long-lasting business relationships.

Conclude and implement the deal

Yesterday we should have closed our current deal – with all that that meant: excitement, perhaps concern, relief and, deep down, great satisfaction. However, an 'agreement in principle' might have been made with the final pressure of some vital details left over to the eleventh hour. Pressure of this kind (against, say, a press conference deadline) could lead to a demand for extra concessions that could change the value of the deal considerably. For all the earlier effort in striking a bargain, negotiators might still find themselves having to split the difference to avoid threats of a walkout.

Your priorities will no doubt have moved on to the next deal. However, the current project will not be successfully completed until the last phase has been carried out in accordance with the specification – and payment has been cleared. It is this stage that will determine the full success of the project.

It can be very difficult for new suppliers to win significant government contracts without a track record. In one case, a supplier offered a very attractive price for innovative software development for a small industry training centre. This puzzled the client, who questioned whether the project could be delivered at the price quoted. However, the contract was delivered successfully and, unbeknown to the first client, the supplier then clinched a much more lucrative contract with a UK government ministry on the strength of that success. The industry training centre had been a 'door-opener'.

A deal is a deal except...

Negotiation meetings are important – they provide opportunities for the parties to test out their arguments, look for common ground, and reach agreement with all the factors needed for the deal to be complete. But this presumes that the deal is enforceable – a factor that may be beyond the negotiator's capacity to assess. Lawyers are highly skilled at exploring such issues, especially ensuring that, in the case of some subsequent dispute, there is an agreement on the chosen jurisdiction of law that will apply.

In commercial agreements involving goods or services, there will normally be a clear statement which defines comprehensive terms and conditions (T&Cs) of the purchase or sale. These are important because, in the case of a dispute, a vital test could be applied to the issue of whose conditions turn out to be superior – and therefore will apply to the agreement.

Returning to practical issues, supposing a verbal agreement has been struck: what if your opponent contacts you to say that something vital has been missed out of the agreement and the case needs to be reopened? Could this be an attempt to try to obtain a better position for them rather than you? Or could it be an opportunity to avoid major embarrassment with a deal that, in truth, is deficient in some way? What action should you take?

In principle, the deal was presumably agreed without any pressure. If so, you might feel that this situation of 'one more discussion' is likely to lead to another and another until your opponent achieves a major improvement in the outcome of the agreement. If there is any evidence of this happening, a meeting could be politely refused. On the other hand, an outright refusal to hear the case – or, at least, to understand what is being queried might seem high-handed. Any subsequent problem could easily have negative repercussions. A careful telephone conversation, in which the plaintiff presents the case, should enable the right decision to be made. If a win-win deal is your ultimate aim, clearly any mistake could poison that collaborative atmosphere.

The situation might be very different if contracts have been signed and exchanged. The legal department would probably need to get involved, and clearly your own credibility will be at stake for not spotting an error before the contract was signed.

Celebrate your success

Most of the work we have discussed this week has assumed that a final agreement or contract will be the final goal. Such a document can be quite complex and, although there will be working papers used to support discussions, it is best practice for the final agreement to be fully detailed – in print – and with all the supporting documents.

> **TIP** *It is essential that the contract matches the verbal agreement – and it must be rigorously checked to ensure that this is the case.*

This is where the documented notes from negotiating meetings are essential. They must reflect the discussions that have occurred and, if they don't, another round of negotiations will certainly be needed.

When a sizeable contract has been agreed, there is sometimes a strong desire among the public-relations community to publicize the good news to the world in general (with a public figure present) – and the markets in particular. This is a natural corollary to all the effort invested in agreeing the contract but it can also create a further 'obstacle course'.

Such an occasion could also cause the client to become a hostage to fortune, as further concessions may be demanded at the eleventh hour before signature is possible. With the clock ticking, and no one wishing to look incompetent in front of the honoured guest and the national or international press, this could provide an opportunistic negotiator with the chance to gain yet more concessions, even after everyone has agreed the final deal.

Monitor progress of implementation

The complex long-term contract you have spent so much time agreeing could marry your and the other party's interests together for some years ahead, so it is important that the agreement includes details on how the progress of implementation will be monitored. This might be achieved by written reports, audits, visits and/or third-party involvement. The commissioning company will almost certainly be expecting to see visible evidence of progress – and such monitoring will most usually be linked to stage payments. More importantly, if visits and reports indicate that progress is slow – or off-course – then corrective action is going to be needed and this must also be negotiated. The implication of this is that it needs to be carried out without conflict or personal unpleasantness. However, it would be worse to allow the deviation to continue only to have to account for an accumulated problem much later on.

It is to be hoped that the contract itself will include provision for the management of any eventual stage failures and how payment will be affected. Failure to include such information in the contract would probably result in another round of negotiation and possibly legal action if agreement could not be reached. This thought concentrates the mind when the parties are concerned with maintaining the original win/win atmosphere that existed when the contract was signed. Now there may be a risk of relations subsiding into blame and counter-blame.

Develop your partnering opportunities and skills

A productive approach for all aspirational negotiators lies in adopting the partnering stance, thereby seeking to grow the business on either side (supplier and client). The rewards will be significant – to both parties. In some instances, this could be a medium- or long-term development of technology that could lead to not inconsiderable wealth. Or it might help ensure that both parties stay in business.

Who is the real client in such a situation? As a supplier, the normal contact person will be the day-to-day client but above this person there will be corporate representatives with whom a supplier may also have infrequent contact. Their loyalty may still, however, be tested in that forum. The temptation to provide uncontrolled (or even critical) feedback needs to be avoided. Trust is everything!

Equally, offering constructive support and suggestions are likely to be increasingly welcomed – especially if these ideas are recycled from current experiences with partners elsewhere. Ultimately, the decision about implementation has to lie with the partner.

An obvious activity where these relationships can become significant occurs when a merger or acquisition is taking place, but such periods can also throw up accusations of partisan and illegal behaviour if the partner's involvement brings intense positive or negative financial effects.

Another partnering opportunity arises when advisers and specialists work together in a consortium (e.g. in an export market); again, care needs to be taken to negotiate the needs of one's own organization with those of other members of the consortium.

Maintain high aspirations

The quality of output is often largely dependent on the personal standards of the individuals involved. These standards have probably been adopted as a result of a wide range of experiences – both good and less successful. It is also a matter of cause and effect – sloppy work can result in poor outcomes.

What is surprising is that so many projects suffer indifferent results, and these must have been foreseen by at least some of those involved, if not the most senior negotiators responsible for setting up the arrangements.

To exploit high aspirations, some organizations benefit from an open management and communication culture so that everyone involved in a project is free to raise critical issues internally if and when the actual performance looks as though it will fall short of the contracted level.

This requires great patience and the ability to provide a listening ear, even for people who might seem unlikeable. Good listening is a rarely taught skill that can be improved. Actually, unlikeable people pose a particular challenge but they can prove remarkably informative if they are approached sensitively.

It is not just sales representatives and buyers who find themselves chasing higher targets year on year; this is a feature of all businesses. So a mark of all negotiators needs to be an understanding of how they can help clients and contacts with the search for continued growth and development. The quid pro quo lies with the return on the investment of time and advice, manifested in increased sales, higher proportional stocks and so on. The point is that business relationships do not stand still – they are subject to the ebb and flow of politics and economics as well as personal credibility. Top negotiators appreciate this. However, it is important that true partners demonstrate continuing care long after a top result on a particular project is achieved.

Monitor and develop your business lifestyle

At the start of the book we introduced the profiling concept and here is an opportunity to revisit those styles. Which did you recognize in yourself? Hopefully, more of your styles belonged to Class A than to Class B.

Class A	Class B
Role 1: Safety First	Role 6: Escapologist
Role 2: Completer/Finisher	Role 7: Politician
Role 3: Expert/Teacher	Role 8: Extrovert
Role 4: Controller	Role 9: Pessimist
Role 5: Opportunist	Role 10: Naive

Plan your future 1

How might you start to change your habitual style? First, we need to identify it and this may require the support of a colleague or manager who can observe a typical meeting and provide some objective feedback. Evidence that points towards any of the Class B categories may need to be addressed; this could benefit from the support of coaching. Another valuable method would be working through a role-play exercise – preferably with the addition of video recording, which will enable further self-analysis.

It should also be remembered that any improvements in style and technique will be noticed by regular opponents, especially if they have benefited from the less effective influencing styles adopted in the past. However, there is an obvious advantage to both participants if negotiations are more effective – and when win/win results occur more naturally.

If you have enjoyed being a fixer of problems that ought to have been predicted from past negotiations, then you are probably leaning towards becoming an Escapologist. You should ask yourself the following questions:

- Do I prefer this way of life? If so, maybe I should be doing something more suited to my limitations.
- Does sorting out crises make me feel good? If they should never have occurred – or you find that the same type of crisis occurs frequently – you should feel disappointed rather than self-satisfied.
- Is your 'busy-ness' secretly criticized by your team, leaving them feeling cynical – or overly casual – as they know that you like to pick up any mistakes
- What changes to the organization would help tighten up decision-making in negotiations? If rearguard negotiating is common in the organization, could this be avoided in the future? Who are the worst offenders and how could they be persuaded and trained to change?
- Does your organization suffer from the phenomenon known as Murphy's Law ('If it can go wrong, it will')? How could the risks of non-compliance be recognized at an earlier stage and avoiding action taken much earlier?
- Does greed figure much in your market or in typical deals?
- Is power misused, causing others to cast around for cost savings that are motivated by the need to survive? How could a more partnering stance be adopted?
- Is the level of detail in research and debate, commitment and delivery consistent and adequate?

- Who applies the 'What if?' questions to your market position? For example: 'What if our current partners went out of business within six months?'; 'What if transportation costs were to double within three months?' and so on. Engaging in blue-sky thinking and contingency planning is very rarely a waste of time.

Knowing something is very different from practising it. Take the opportunity to re-examine your normal behaviour. Don't ask yourself 'Is this a new idea?'; ask yourself 'Do I do this? And, if not, how could I adopt this method with sufficient confidence to succeed? Have I prepared a personal action plan (including some personal feedback) to underwrite change and achieve the personal improvements I know are desirable/essential?'

Plan your future 2

If you are trying to improve your involvement in more advanced negotiations, the following checklists of self-development skills will help:

Tips for listening

Try not to:

- **make hasty judgements,** such as tuning out because you believe the speaker has nothing interesting to say; condemning a subject as uninteresting without giving it a fair hearing; or jumping the gun on what you think is about to come in conversation
- **let your attention wander** – avoid getting easily distracted by other sights and sounds around you and try not to show any unwitting signs of impatience or irritation
- **listen selectively,** by turning a deaf ear to certain topics; only listening to certain people; wanting to hear only about the good things and not the bad; letting someone's delivery pull you off listening to what they have to say.

Tips for improving your assertiveness

Do you:

- think before speaking, thus improving confidence by eliminating ums and ers?
- maintain a firm, confident tone of voice in meetings?
- say what you mean without waffling?
- show positive body language to support a businesslike image?
- avoid apologetic behaviour?

Plan your future 3

Extroverts with huge amounts of self-confidence tend to rise to the top of the sales profession and often transfer across into buying/purchasing and line management roles. However, they may also continue to use the habitual talk/listen ratios that have helped them to be successful in the past. This may not be the most effective style to use and, if only one resolution is likely to help anyone in this position, it is this: *ask more questions*.

It would be simplistic to say that questions merely bring answers; they also buy thinking/planning time and allow the questioner to gain control (as the opponent loses thinking time because they are busy deciding how to answer the questions that have been fired at them).

Extroverts are notable for talking too much; they may unwittingly give away vital bargaining information without obtaining anything in return. So, asking more questions, designed to tie the conversation down to the case in hand and the vital factors, is extremely important.

In the longer term, your reputation will have been considerably enhanced and you should be actively considering how to build on your success. There is probably no better way to improve one's future prospects than by being attached to a large and successful project – and so it should not come as any surprise if a job offer or two starts to arrive.

The biggest trap for experienced negotiators is complacency – it is easy to draw out the successful projects but what about the rest? It is a challenging but exciting role that can bring great satisfaction – but only if negotiators avoid those tempting shortcuts. Once you have polished your skills in current roles and projects, you may feel that it is important to maintain the sense of personal challenge by applying them in new sectors. After a number of projects have completed successfully, larger schemes will probably open up. However, successful completion is most likely to be the determining success factor when it comes to new appointments. It would be wrong to prejudge here the attraction of such approaches, regardless of how attractive they may appear to be. The right time to be thinking of moving on (if at all) is when the current project is successfully completed.

Good negotiators are always in demand. Keep growing – and try to ensure that you share your experience with younger, less experienced negotiators around you!

If you are inclined to give something back, experienced negotiators are needed all round the planet, often in areas where the necessary level of investment may be impossible to achieve. In such situations monetary benefit may be poor, but the opportunities for great personal satisfaction from seeing good charitable works succeed could bring an even higher level of satisfaction.

Summary

It would be a strange but perfect world if every negotiator were able to claim that all their negotiation outcomes were perfect and all implementation occurred exactly as agreed. However, unfortunately the world is not perfect and it is vital that experienced negotiators continue to learn and grow from each project they undertake. Making mistakes is human – but repeating the same mistakes and *not* learning from them is inexcusable.

This book should have pinpointed best practices and prompted you to identify keys to enhanced negotiation that simply require your motivation and determination to implement – which is why we have included a framework of a Personal Action Plan at the end of this book. By now, this should feature at least seven action points that you should be able to implement.

If you have found any more improvement points, try to prioritize them and introduce them steadily, monitoring their success as you go. And remember that you might well negotiate with others who are trying to implement their own action plans. Collaborative negotiation is, as this book willl have shown you, all about achieving win/win.

Progress check (answers at the back)

1. Major stand-alone contracts should be negotiated hard in order to:
a) Ensure the very best benefits are gained, together with punitive compensation (just in case) ❑
b) Enable the two organizations to grow together ❑
c) Ensure that the parties can prove competence should the details become public ❑
d) Prove that the deal has been struck by competent negotiators ❑

2. The final negotiation phase will benefit from:
a) Scrutiny by a third party not previously involved in the discussions ❑
b) An escape clause in case of undisclosed matters ❑
c) Legal protection against fraud or exaggerated claims ❑
d) Confidential advisers to ensure the deal can be fully implemented ❑

3. A pre-booked press event brings:
a) Potential image problems should agreement be delayed ❑
b) Guaranteed column inches for an agreed deal ❑
c) The risk that one party will hold the other hostage ❑
d) The best target for closure of the negotiation ❑

4. Legal advice for a negotiation team approaching closure is:
a) Vital, to ensure any agreement is enforceable ❑
b) An item that should be included in the final budget ❑
c) A service that should be available to both sides ❑
d) An essential feature of a win/win deal ❑

5. Negotiating in a team requires:
a) Self-control and discipline against the risk of multi-speak ❑
b) A sense of mission and self-belief ❑
c) Defence/attack if and when necessary ❑
d) Maintaining loyalty to the team and its objectives ❑

6. The best profile for a negotiator to adopt for high-value contracts in the long term would be:
a) Opportunist ❑
b) Expert/teacher ❑
c) Completer/finisher ❑
d) Pessimist ❑

7. The best action to take when there is overt disagreement within your negotiating team is to:
a) Provide a distraction by changing the subject ❑
b) Call a recess ❑
c) Pass a note to the 'guilty' party ❑
d) Invoke the team manifesto ❑

SUNDAY MONDAY TUESDAY WEDNESDAY THURSDAY FRIDAY SATURDAY

8. A lot of counter-proposing is:
a) A sign of a win/lose culture between negotiators ❑
b) A risk that could lead to defence/attack cycles ❑
c) A hint that agreement will be impossible ❑
d) An indicator of a very competitive negotiator ❑

9. The biggest trap for experienced negotiators is:
a) Talking in an uncontrolled way ❑
b) Over-confidence and complacency ❑
c) Making assumptions ❑
d) Failure to do one's homework ❑

10. Negotiating skills should be seen as:
a) Vital skills to help survive and grow in everyday life ❑
b) Showing opponents that you mean business ❑
c) A way of avoiding win/lose outcomes ❑
d) Solely the province of commerce and industry ❑

7 × 7

Seven key ideas

1 Develop (or reinforce) your self-confidence to negotiate – especially when working in an environment that does not seem to be conducive to negotiating.

2 Relax your style! If you have prepared thoroughly, discussion, proposing and agreeing should be possible without tension, embarrassment or aggression.

3 Fix your negotiation 'zones'. Least and most favourable boundaries should be set before a meeting... by both sides!

4 Use 'small-talk' but avoid 'loose talk' (which may give away vital information which strengthens your opponent's position).

5 Praise opponents' flexibility and reward it with small concessions that should help to build the feeling of 'win/win'.

6 Impress opponents with your command of your subject – but don't let this turn into a competition about who knows most.

7 Don't make 'cast iron claims' about exaggerated points – this risks your credibility (even if you later accept that you have made a mistake and back down).

Seven key resources for the negotiator

1 Numeracy!
2 Computer skills
3 Research
4 Determination
5 Self-belief/confidence
6 Building the 'winning' team
7 Finishing (realism)

Seven best personal resources

1 *Confidence: How winning streaks and losing streaks begin and end* by Rosabeth Moss Kanter (Three Rivers Press, 2006)

2 *Eyes Wide Open: How to make smart decisions in a confusing world* by Noreena Hertz (William Collins, 2013)

3 *Emotional Intelligence Workbook: Take practical steps to improve* by Jill and Derek Dann (Hodder & Stoughton, 2012)

4 *Manipulating Meetings: How to get what you want, when you want it* by David Martin (3rd edn, Prentice Hall, 1999)

5 *Conflicts: A better way to resolve them* by Edward de Bono (Penguin, 1991)

6 *'I'm OK – You're OK'* by Thomas A. Harris (Arrow, 2012)

7 *NLP: The new technology of achievement* by Steve Andreas and Charles Faulkner (Nicholas Brealey, 1996) Plus a bonus... *The Negotiation Coach* by Peter Fleming (John Murray Learning, 2015) (Provides a comprehensive menu of self-development and and improvement activities.)

Seven things to do today

1 Review your current practices and build a new action plan.
2 Invest time in relation to potential pay-off in terms of technique and results.
3 Build your team by sharing insights and skills and being prepared to delegate the progressive projects to trusted people.
4 Involve others in difficult cases to maintain open-mindedness about alternative solutions and provide learning opportunities for the team.
   Check it all out! Especially those complex schemes...
5 Will it work? Does it meet all the promises you/they are making?
6 How does it feel to do 'business' with your 'opponent'? And how might it feel for them to do business with you?
7 Is that consistent with other departments/functions/levels of authority? If not, what can be done about it?

Seven inspiring negotiation strategies

1 'You are not in a negotiating position – please leave!' A very successful head of a renowned academic institution used this combative approach to buy time – a strong bargaining tactic within his own team that restricted time-wasting debate on poorly thought-out schemes.

2 Top lawyers may exploit their 'bargaining positions' by applying an authoritative air that adds weight to all that they say. This can be difficult to break down (in court or in commercial bargaining) because it is based on thorough, and very pointed, questioning!

3 'Negotiation is important because in engaging with someone with a different perspective, you can more easily identify the questions you need to consider in order to improve yourself and your own position.' Alastair, Bishop of Derby

4 Internal negotiations are strongly influenced by political and power relations between competing departments and functions. Top managers quickly form 'unwritten rules' for bargaining, which may include: 'Don't bring me problems – only solutions' or 'No nasty surprises, thank you!'

5 The late Lord Mottistone, (first director of the British Industrial Training Board for Distribution) shared his charismatic personality with liberal/public praise for the efforts of all those who deserved it. Praise is a strong motivator and one that can generate further out-of-the-ordinary efforts and results.

6 Founder of two pioneering banks, Mike Harris is now a mentor for other pioneers. His mantra is: 'So many leadership conversations are, in fact, a negotiation. You are trying to find the common ground where it is in *their* interest to give you what *you need from them*.'

7 'Negotiating in the Sales and Marketing function often revolves around price ... The consequence of a generous discount can directly affect bottom-line profits whereas quality, value and service build a strong and profitable business.' Ron Coleman, founder of Invicta Training

Seven negotiation quotes

1 'You must never try to make all the money that's in a deal. Let the other fellow make some money too, because if you have a reputation for always making all the money, you won't have many deals.' J. Paul Getty

2 'Anger can be an effective negotiating tool, but only as a calculated act, never as a reaction.' Mark McCormack

3 'When a man says that he approves something in principle, it means he hasn't the slightest intention of putting it into practice.' Otto von Bismarck

4 'If you come to a negotiation table saying you have the final truth, that you know nothing but the truth and that is final, you will get nothing.' Harri Holkeri

5 'Diplomacy is the art of letting someone else have your way.' Sir David Frost

6 'The first principle of contract negotiation is don't remind them of what you did in the past; tell them what you're going to do in the future.' Stan Musial

7 'There's no road map on how to raise a family: it's always an enormous negotiation!' Meryl Streep

Seven trends for tomorrow

1 Continuing greater use of non-personal methods of communicating (i.e. use of media, text exchange, etc.), *leading to...*

2 Greater opportunities for exploiting personality and the 'touch and feel' of personal face-to-face communicating.

3 More timely communicating – more strictly focused (but 'disguised' as social entertainment?).

4 Power and authority more tightly focused in fewer hands (with concentration of business wealth and opportunity), *possibly leading to...*

5 Increased opportunities through niche business/organizations with new start-ups by individualistic entrepreneurs, *and*

6 Greater collaborative business initiatives in unusual sectors, such as lifestyle operations (e.g. fast cars; the rebuilding of heritage vehicles), stimulating cohorts of traditional and new skills centres.

7 Meantime, continuing volume business pressure based on price and value for money operations with the emphasis on quantities and inexpensive prices (mainly through energetic agents representing low price/value world economies – dependent on continuing stable political/economic positions). An obvious outcome here will be the requirement for more international negotiators with sensitivity and competence in cross-border and political/cultural negotiations.

Answers to progress checks

Sunday: 1d; 2c; 3d; 4c; 5c; 6d; 7a; 8d; 9a; 10d

Monday: 1d; 2c; 3c; 4c; 5d; 6b; 7a; 8a; 9c; 10c

Tuesday: 1d; 2d; 3c; 4b; 5d; 6d; 7a; 8a; 9a; 10a

Wednesday: 1d; 2d; 3c; 4b; 5d; 6d; 7a; 8a; 9a; 10a

Thursday: 1d; 2d; 3c; 4b; 5d; 6d; 7a; 8a; 9a; 10a

Friday: 1c; 2d; 3b; 4a; 5a; 6b; 7b; 8c; 9b; 10d

Saturday: 1a; 2d; 3c; 4a; 5a; 6c; 7b; 8d; 9b; 10c

Personal Action Plan

Objective	Target Date	Completed
1		
2		
3		
4		
5		
6		
7		
8		